Arkansas History

Arkansas History: A Journey through Time

The Growth of the Twenty-Fifth State of the Union from 1833 to 1957

Arlen Jones

ARKANSAS HISTORY: A JOURNEY THROUGH TIME
The Growth of the Twenty-Fifth State of the Union from 1833 to 1957

iUniverse books may be ordered through booksellers or by contacting:

iUniverse
1663 Liberty Drive
Bloomington, IN 47403
www.iuniverse.com
1-800-Authors (1-800-288-4677)

Because of the dynamic nature of the Internet, any web addresses or links contained in this book may have changed since publication and may no longer be valid. The views expressed in this work are solely those of the author and do not necessarily reflect the views of the publisher, and the publisher hereby disclaims any responsibility for them.

Any people depicted in stock imagery provided by Thinkstock are models, and such images are being used for illustrative purposes only. Certain stock imagery © Thinkstock.

ISBN: 978-1-4917-7636-0 (sc)
ISBN: 978-1-4917-7637-7 (hc)
ISBN: 978-1-4917-7638-4 (e)

Library of Congress Control Number: 2015914667

Print information available on the last page.

iUniverse rev. date: 10/07/2015

About the Author

Arlen Jones earned his Bachelor of Arts Degree from the University of Arkansas at Pine Bluff in Pine Bluff, Arkansas, and his master of science in education from Ouachita Baptist University in Arkadelphia, Arkansas. He earned additional hours in school administration from the University of Central Arkansas in Conway, Arkansas. He served as state director of the Federal Program at the Arkansas Department of Education in Little Rock, Arkansas, where he retired after twenty-eight years of employment. Arlen has also served as department chair of social studies and taught social science at Arkansas Baptist College in Little Rock, Arkansas, for fifteen years. During his tenure, he received a certificate of recognition for outstanding and devoted services to the student body and the teacher of the year award.

Arlen is a retired military personal officer after twenty-three years of service. Arlen and his wife, Joyce, are the parents of one daughter, Arlinda Joyce Jones.

Dedication

I am dedicating this book in honor of my father, Reverend Doctor Floyd Osbourne Jones, who was the guiding force in my life. He believed it was important for young people to have a positive place in culture and that young Arkansans should take pride in their state history.

Dr. Jones was born on January 9, 1912, to Reverend Stephen B. Jones and Mrs. Mary Ella Jane Goods Jones in Thornton, Arkansas. Dr. Jones attended Thornton Public Schools, where he graduated, and attended Arkansas Baptist College in Little Rock, where he graduated at the top of his class (summa cum laude). Dr. Jones received his masters in religion studies from Bishop College, which was at the time located in Marshall, Texas. Bishop College was the premier school for the training of African American ministers for many years. Dr. Jones later received an honorary doctor of divinity from Arkansas Baptist College.

During World War II, Dr. Jones was drafted to the US Navy. He served aboard the USS *Knox* (APA-46). He was engaged in ten naval battles. During his stay in the navy, Dr. Jones was able to travel to Cuba, Africa, Asia, China, and other islands. His travels totaled more than ninety thousand miles. In 1945 he helped to organize the First Christian Association South of the Equator.

Dr. Jones's teaching experience consisted of being employed as a classroom teacher at the Calhoun County Training School, which was located in Thornton, Arkansas, and Sparkman Public Schools in Sparkman, Arkansas. In later years, he served as a principal of Sparkman Elementary School, as well as a member of the trustee board of Arkansas Baptist College.

As Longfellow said, "Lives of great men all remind us, we can make our lives sublime, and departing, leave behind us, footprints on the sands of time." Dr. Jones has left some indelible footprints in Calhoun County and made his own mark on Arkansas history.

Contents

Introduction

Why use primary documents during instruction?

Teaching with primary documents encourages a varied learning environment for teachers and students. Analysis of documents, independent research, and group work become a gateway for research with historical records in ways that sharpen student skills and enthusiasm for history and language arts. Analyzing primary documents allows students to examine relationships between national, state, and local history. These documents allow students to experience history instead of reading about it in a traditional textbook.

What does this publication offer students?

This publication provides a journey through time that a traditional textbook cannot offer. It is Arkansas history waiting to be explored. The expedition follows documents that connect Arkansas before it was a state and then the chronology of statehood. This collection is also filled with authentic photos, maps, and ads of early Arkansas. Areas of focus are listed below.

- Arkansas before it was a state
- How Arkansas became a state
- A free state or not?
- The constitutional convention
- Work of the legislature
- Candidates for president in 1836
- Statehood and politics

How is this unit of study relevant to instruction in my classroom?

This unit of study is correlated with the Arkansas state standards for social studies for grades six through twelve, common core state standards for English/language arts for grades six through twelve, and Arkansas history for grades seven and eight.

A special note to teachers:

The spelling, syntax, and sentence structure are all captured from the original selected pieces written from the historical time period of the *Arkansas Gazette*, State Centennial Edition, Little Rock, Arkansas, June 15, 1936, Volume 117 to Volume 209. The lack of contemporary writing is due to the fact that this book has been created with materials to provide teachers and students realistic prospective of the era. Please discuss this with your students when exploring the primary documents. It is very important to address how the language and expectations of editing has changed over the years.

Chronology of Statehood

1833—Ben Desha advocated statehood in his race against Ambrose H. Sevier for delegate in Congress. Sevier took the position that the time was not opportune. Sevier was elected.

1833—December 17, Ambrose H. Sevier, delegate in Congress, introduced a bill in the House for a census in Arkansas to determine whether the territory was eligible for statehood. (The state census was finally used.)

1834—Statehood was advocated in letters in the press and at meetings in various counties.

1834—December 17, Ambrose H. Sevier, delegate in Congress, having heard that the territory of Michigan was to apply for admission to the Union, introduced a resolution in the House, which was adopted, instructing the House Committee on Territories to consider the expediency of Arkansas's admission.

1834—March 11, the House Committee on Territories reported against Mr. Sevier's resolution (see December 17, 1834) but reported a bill for a census.

1834—May 2, Mr. Tipton reported to the Senate a bill for the admission of Arkansas (and Michigan). It was amended to provide for a census.

December 1834–March 1835—Arkansas and Michigan statehood bills failed passage at the "short session" of the twenty-third Congress.

1835—August 3, more than two-thirds of each house of the legislature, chosen in the territorial election, was for statehood. The regular territorial census taken in this year showed a population of 51,809, which qualified Arkansas for statehood.

1835—August 1, Governor William Savin Fulton of Arkansas Territory held in an address to the people that Congress must first give authority for the territorial legislature to provide for a convention to form a constitution.

1835—August 10, Governor Fulton sent to John Forsyth, secretary of state of the United States, copies of his address to the people of Arkansas on the statehood question and asked for advice on the course he should follow.

1835—September 21, B. F. Butler, attorney general of the United States, held in an opinion requested by Secretary of State Forsyth at the direction of President Andrew Jackson that the people of Arkansas might petition Congress for admission to the Union and Congress might accept a proposed constitution.

1835—October 5, territorial legislature met and passed a bill (House, 27–7; Council, 17–11) for a Constitutional convention. It became law without Governor Fulton's signature.

1835—December 5, Constitutional Convention delegates were elected. The popular vote was largely in favor of statehood.

1836—January 4, the Constitutional Convention met at Little Rock. It adopted the proposed state constitution on January 30 by a vote of forty-seven to four.

1836—March 10, President Andrew Jackson submitted the proposed Arkansas constitution to Congress.

1836—March 22, Senator James Buchanan reported a bill to provide for admission of Arkansas.

1836—April 4, the Senate adopted the bill for Arkansas's admission.

1836—June 6, the House adopted Mr. Sevier's resolution to consider until disposed of bills for admission of Arkansas (and Michigan).

1836—June 13, the House adopted bills for the admission of Arkansas (and Michigan).

1836—June 15, President Andrew Jackson signed the bills for the admission of Arkansas (and Michigan).

1836—July 4, the twenty-fifth star, for Arkansas, was added to the US flag.

Chronology after Statehood

1836—James Conway was elected first governor.

1838—A steam-powered ferry began operating in Little Rock.

1840—The Federal government began construction of its Arsenal in Little Rock.

1846—Congress declared war on Mexico. Arkansas raised a regiment of volunteer cavalry commanded by Archibald Yell.

1853—Arkansas's first railroad, the Arkansas Central, was chartered by the legislature.

1858—*The Arkansas Traveler* was published.

1859—The School for the Blind was authorized by the state assembly.

1861—On May 20 Arkansas was admitted into the Confederate States of America.

1862—The battles of Pea Ridge and Prairie Ridge were fought. The Union won both fights.

1863—Federal troops occupied most of Arkansas.

1864—Teenaged Confederate David O. Dodd was executed by feds for spying.

1865—The Union government became the sole governing group in Arkansas.

1868—Ku Klux Klan protests led to thirteen counties being placed under martial law.

1872—The Arkansas Industrial University, a land grant school, opened in Fayetteville.

1874—Reconstruction ended in Arkansas. President Ulysses Grant recognized Republican Elijah Baxter as governor.

1877—Hot Springs National Park was established as the Hot Springs Reservation.

1883—The Mosaic Templars was founded in Little Rock and eventually spread to twenty-six states.

1888—Bauxite was mined in Saline County.

1891—The first Jim Crow law in Arkansas was enacted: the Separate Coach law. The law segregated blacks and whites on trains.

1894—Arkansas's first night baseball game was played in Little Rock's West End Park.

1898—Two Arkansas infantries were called into service in the war against Spain.

1900—The cornerstone of the new state capitol building is laid on the grounds of the former state penitentiary.

1903—*On a Slow Train Through Arkansas* was published.

1906—Diamonds were discovered in Pike County.

1907—Arkansas coal mines produced more than 2,750,000 tons of coal.

1915—Statewide prohibition went into effect, and the state capitol building was completed.

1917—Seventy-two thousand Arkansans served in World War I.

1919—Race riot occurred in Elaine. Black and white Arkansas was further divided.

1921—Oil was found near Smackover.

1922—The radio station WOK began broadcasting in Pine Bluff.

1925—A woman's right to vote went into effect after Brickhouse v. Hill.

1927—Severe flooding destroyed farmlands.

1931—Nearly half of Arkansas business that was operating before the 1929 stock market crash was closed.

1932—Hattie Caraway became the first woman elected to the US Senate.

1936—The Waterbury Clock Company, later renamed Timex, opened in Little Rock.

1939—The Magnet Cove Barium Corporation began mining in Saline County.

1941—Louise Loughborough's preservation charities led to the opening of the Arkansas Territorial Capitol Restoration, later renamed the Historic Arkansas Museum. World War II broke out and two hundred thousand Arkansans served in the military.

1942—Japanese Americans were held in internment camps near Jerome and Rohwer, Arkansas.

1944—J. William Fulbright was elected to the US Senate.

1946—Decorated Marine Sidney P. McMath was elected Garland County prosecuting attorney.

1948—Sid McMath was elected governor. McMath placed African Americans on the state boards for the first time since Reconstruction.

1955—Orval Fabus was elected governor.

1957—The Little Rock Central High School crisis brought international attention to the American civil rights movement and divided races in Arkansas.

Chapter 1

Arkansas before Statehood

The purchase of Louisiana from France by the United States for $11,250,000 was consummated on October 31, 1803. It was then that President Thomas Jefferson approved of the treaty of purchase, as ratified by Congress, together with an act of Congress, authorizing him to "take possession of Louisiana and form a temporary government therein." For its immediate and temporary government, the purchased territory was divided into two parts. All the land north of the present state of Louisiana was designated as the District of Louisiana. The United States, through its agent, Major Amos Stoddard of the US Army, actually took possession of this section of the purchase at St. Louis on March 10, 1804. At that time the district, which was regarded as unorganized territory, was attached temporarily to the Indiana Territory, of which General William Henry Harrison was governor. About a year later the name District of Louisiana was changed to Territory of Louisiana, and as such, the whole of Upper Louisiana, as the district was popularly known, was divorced from Indian Territory and given a territorial government of its own.

President Jefferson, on March 3, 1805, appointed General James Wilkinson of the US Army governor of Louisiana Territory. A territorial legislature, composed of the governor and the territorial judges, was convened at St. Louis, and there, on June 26, 1806, the legislature created the District of Arkansas. This embraced nearly all the present state of Arkansas, together with the greater part of Oklahoma. On March 3, 1807, General Wilkinson was succeeded as the governor of the Louisiana Territory by Captain Meriwether Lewis, and on August 23, 1808, Governor Lewis appointed the following officers for the government of the District of Arkansas: Harold Stillwell, sheriff; John W. Honey, judge of Probate; Joseph Stillwell, Francis Vaugine, and

Benjamin Foy, judges of the Court of Common Pleas; Perley Wallis, deputy attorney general of the district; and Andrew Fagot, justice of the peace. Judge Honey held his first session of court on December 12, 1808, at Arkansas Post, then the seat of government for the district.

In the fall of 1809, Governor Lewis died in Tennessee while en route to Washington; he was succeeded by Benjamin A. Howard of Kentucky. It was during the administration of Governor Howard (1810–1812) that the New Madrid earthquake all but destroyed the village of New Madrid and left sunken, overflowed areas in the northeast corner of the District of Arkansas.

Congress changed the name of Louisiana Territory to Missouri Territory on June 4, 1812, following the admission of the southern part of the Louisiana Purchase to the Union as the state of Louisiana. On October 1, 1812, Governor Howard issued a proclamation changing the five districts of the Missouri Territory into counties and the legislature into an elective body of two houses: a Council and a House of Representatives. Arkansas Post was continued as the seat of government in Arkansas County. The first popular election in the territory was held on November 9, 1812. Edward Hempstead was chosen as the territorial delegate to Congress, and representatives from the several counties to the House in the legislature were also elected. Arkansas County, though it was not given a House member all its own, was represented jointly with New Madrid County by Samuel Phillips and John Shrader. Governor Fredrick Bates called the newly elected members of the House of Representatives into session on December 7, 1812, and they nominated persons for appointment or confirmation by the president of the United States to membership in the Council, or Senate, of the legislature. While the House and the acting governor were waiting for President James Madison to pass on and confirm the election of the personnel of the Council, the new governor of the territory, William Clark, younger brother of George Rogers Clark, arrived at St. Louis and started his duties.

Governor Clark called the legislature, or General Assembly as it was officially named, together for July 5, 1813. The boundaries of Arkansas County were defined by an act of this legislature as "all that part of Missouri Territory south of New Madrid County." The same act further provided that thereafter the county of Arkansas should elect its own separate representative in the House. A census of the territory was ordered, and when completed, it showed Arkansas County as having a male population of voting age of 827.

Meanwhile, Congress passed an act requiring that two terms of Superior Court, the US territorial court, be held "in each and every year at the Village of Arkansas." The same act further provided for the appointment of an additional territorial judge, who was required to reside "at or near the Village of Arkansas." To this office President Madison appointed George Bullit, of Ste. Genevieve County, on February 9, 1814. Judge Bullit promptly moved with his family to Arkansas Post, where he stayed in office until 1819. During the five years of his residence at the Post, the territory now embraced in the state of Arkansas was redivided into five counties by the Missouri legislature and Bullit organized local government in all of them.

At the second session of the Missouri General Assembly, Arkansas County had its own representative in the person of Henry Cassidy. It was during this session, on January 15, 1815, that the county of Lawrence was created, out of territory now partly in Arkansas and partly in Missouri.

The fourth and last territorial legislature of Missouri formed on December 15, 1818. It consisted of three new counties—Pulaski, Clark, and Hempstead—from about three-fourths of the area of Arkansas County. These three counties, together with Arkansas and Lawrence, were erected into the new Territory of Arkansas by an act of Congress approved March 2, 1819. The next day, March 3, 1819, President James Monroe appointed General James Miller of New Hampshire and

Robert Crittenden of Kentucky as governor and secretary, respectively, of Arkansas Territory. July 4, 1819, began its separate existence. On the day appointed, Robert Crittenden, already on the scene, entered upon his duties as secretary and acting governor at Arkansas Post, which had been made the temporary seat of the territorial government. Governor Miller did not reach the Post until December 26, 1819.

The first Arkansas legislature convened at Arkansas Post on July 28, 1819. It was composed of the acting governor, Robert Crittenden, and the judges of the territorial Superior Court: Charles Jouett, Robert P. Letcher, and Andrew Scott. The legislature completed its work in five days and adjourned on August 3. At the insistence of Robert Crittenden, a general election was held on November 20. James Woodson Bates was elected territorial delegate to Congress; members of the first General Assembly—a Council and House of Representatives—were also elected. On that same day, November 20, 1819, William E. Woodruff printed at Arkansas Post the first issue of the *Arkansas Gazette*.

On January 27, 1819, the day after his arrival in Arkansas, Governor Miller called an extraordinary session of the General Assembly for February 7, 1820, at Arkansas Post. The session lasted two weeks, until February 24, when it took a recess, planning to meet again on October 2, 1820. At this adjourned session, the legislature passed an act making Little Rock the permanent seat of the territorial government and appointed June 1, 1921, as the date when the act of removal would be effective.

The second General Assembly, the first to sit at Little Rock, convened October 1, 1921. Robert Crittenden was again acting governor because of the absence of Governor Miller. Henry W. Conway had succeeded James Woodson Bates as the delegate to Congress. During the month of December in 1821, William E. Woodruff moved his printing press from Arkansas Post to Little Rock. By the beginning of 1822, Little Rock had grown from a clearing for a town site, with but a single shack of two rooms on it in July 1820, into a village of about a dozen houses, which were mostly built of logs.

Governor Miller, who bought a farm and built a residence on it at Crystal Hill, about twelve miles up the Arkansas River from Little Rock, held the office of governor until December 1824. He was succeeded in 1825 by General George Izard of South Carolina. Robert Crittenden continued as secretary of the territory under Izard. On October 29, Crittenden and Henry W. Conway, the delegate to Congress, fought a duel across the Mississippi from the mouth of White River; Conway was mortally wounded and died a few days later.

Chapter 2

<u>How Arkansas Became a State</u>

Just when the aspiration that Arkansas might take her place as a great American commonwealth first stirred the imagination of the dreamer of dreams can never be known. This much, however, we do know: as early as 1831, the vision of statehood floated like a cloud suffused with the roseate hues of the dawn before the prophetic eyes of Desha and Crittenden—a vision which neither of them lived to see realized.

In the campaign between Desha and Sevier for the election of a delegate to Congress, Desha stated that when Arkansas had the population required by law, he would, as a citizen, advocate the propriety of her entering the Union of states as soon as she could form her constitution and obtain the assent of the federal government. He pointed out that the delegate in Congress from the territory could not act, even after the territory possessed the requisite numbers, without "the expression of the will of a majority of the people made by a petition to Congress directly or through their legislature." The statehood issue was also made the topic of several communications appearing in the *Advocate,* which contained Desha's circular.

Sevier's views at that time were sufficiently set forth in his circular of April 11, 1831. He stated that the territory did not possess sufficient population to entitle it to admission into the Union. He said that, should immigration continue as it had done for the two or three years proceeding, the territory would shortly have it in its power "to enjoy the benefits of such a government." Until then the agitation of this "excitable question was premature. When we are out of debt and when we have the population and the means to support a state government, I am as anxious as the most impatient to see this territory become a state."

And then there was a lull. There was no reference to statehood in the four-column circular of Robert Crittenden in the *Advocate* of April 17, 1833, in which he announced himself a candidate for Congress against Sevier, and in which he set forth fully his connection with Arkansas affairs from 1819. Nor does it seem that either Crittenden or Sevier alluded to the subject in their canvass.

The scene shifted to Washington.

To Realize Her Destiny

William E. Woodruff, editor of the *Arkansas Gazette,* had this to say:

As you invite your friends to a temperate discussion of a state government, in your paper of the twenty-first instant, I beg you to suggest an idea or two. The resolution submitted by Mr. Sevier to the House of Representatives, which was adopted, instructing the Committee on the Territories to inquire into the expediency permitting the people of Arkansas to form a state government, and for her admission into the Union on an equal footing with the original states, is marked by a wise and prudent foresight, as well as by a cautious circumspection on the part of Mr. Sevier. The step is an important one, and though the cooperation of the Legislature, and the expressed instructions of the people, would relieve him from a weight of responsibility, I doubt whether a different course would exonerate him the censure of his constituents. They place him at Washington as their sentinel and invest him with discretion to do what may appear to him to be for their interests.

Mr. Sevier says, "Michigan will of course be a free state, and should she go into the Union as such, the happy balance of political power now existing in the Senate will be destroyed, unless a slave state should go in with her." This reasoning of Mr. Sevier's appears to me conclusive; for an evenly balanced Senate, for and against slavery, will preserve and secure to us sources of wealth and future greatness. Arkansas is perfectly accessible to emigration, or will be in short time, by land and water. The great Memphis road will be shortly constructed, and an appropriation will be made this session for the removal of the obstruction for the Red River raft. As a territorial government, immigration would have no security for the removal of their Negro property. But let Arkansas be admitted into the Union as a slave State, and then will she have some security and a taxable influx of wealth and population that, together with the percentage on the sales of the public lands and the absolute grant of our salines, will yield her revenue sufficient to meet the contingent expenses of a state government. Let it be recollected that the southern and eastern parts of Arkansas are admirably adapted to the culture of cotton. The cold and unproductive lands of North Arkansas and West Tennessee; the sterility of the Carolinas; the somewhat rebellious spirit of Georgia; and the disaffection of the Negroes in Virginia and Maryland will induce people, with and without Negroes, to migrate to Arkansas from even the shores of the Atlantic Ocean, as well as for the benefit of pastures as that their Negro labor and industry will be available to them. Those circumstances combined furnish evidence to my mind that Arkansas will emerge from weakness to strength, from poverty to wealth. As she increases in population, so will she increase in riches in a like ratio or proportion.

With respect to appropriations for internal improvements, I would remark that so soon as the national debt is extinguished, the revenue will be graduated to meet the current expenses of the government, so that the Government will not long have it in her power to extend appropriations of favor to us. She has been liberal already to profusion, and when we see her power diminished, let us escape from the fetters of childhood for the purpose of exercising a democratic voice in the councils of the nation, for the preservation of the Union, the envy of the world, and the proud inheritance of every honest American.[1]

Government Has Been Good to Us

Mr. Woodruff went on to write the following:

That Arkansas should go into a state government appears to me desirable, for I do not like her utter dependence on the general government and her being obliged to receive the latter's dictation, without a vote in what may, or may not, be for her good.

True it is, that the Federal Government has fostered and protected Arkansas with a peculiar tenderness and paternal care, for which she owes her the same filial obligation of love and duty that children owe to their parents. She has, besides, extended to Arkansas an unparalleled degree of munificence as a part or portion of her patrimony, as you please. Yet, it ill comports with the genius and the free institutions of the American people to remain beyond a given time in a state of insecurity and nonage. Where we are not contributors, let us no longer be clogs and sturdy beggars. Let us set up for ourselves; let us be the pioneers of our own destiny, and try our capacity at self-government, as an integral part of this great Confederacy.

A state government might be considered somewhat premature but for the admission of Michigan as a free state into the Union, a circumstance which induces the precipitation of Arkansas into it at this time also. For if the balance or

---

1   William E. Woodruff, *Arkansas Gazette State Centennial Edition,* June 15, 1936.

equilibrium is once lost in the National Senate, in favor of the free states, the loss will be irreparable. No territory can be subsequently admitted into the Union as a slave state. No future legislation can ever reach or repair it while the Senate of the United States, a strong coordinate branch of the national legislature, possesses the power of putting a negative spin on it.

Arkansas is favored by Providence with a mild and genial climate. The industrious, rich, and poor are amply compensated for their labors. The seasons are certain, and some parts of it are well suited to the cultivation of cotton. The northern and western sections of it produce small grain of every variety and in quantity and quality equal to any in the world. Summer and winter cattle ranges abound everywhere. A well-flavored grape grows in spontaneous abundance throughout the territory; and the German emigrants say that with a proper degree of attention to the treatment of the vine in Arkansas, as good wine can be made from it as they ever saw anywhere on the banks of the Rhine in Europe. Arkansas, when she becomes a state, with her local advantages of climate, soil, and navigation, with her general adaptation to the growth and production of the staple commodities of the western country, and with a constitution based on principles of common sense and justice, will be sought after with as much avidity as ever the land of Canaan was by the Israelites under the guidance of Moses and his rod in the days of yore. Arkansas, in process of time (a short time too), will provide for her own consumption and export cotton, flour, corn, beef, pork, lard, wine, peltries, and various other kickshaws, which will bring men, money, and other taxable luxuries into the country.

While slavery does exist in our government and the people have their property invested in slaves, my humble opinion is that we had better go into a slave state government while we have an opportunity. For if ever those humane philanthropists—as the antislavery men call themselves—get the ascendancy in Congress, they will sound their tocsin of alarm and agitate the question of slave emancipation. And then what will the probable result be? Why it will be a total abolition of slavery, and as a consequence growing out of it, a dissolution of the Union. If the people were paid an indemnity for their slaves, it would be well enough to abolish slavery. But the government cannot indemnify slave holders with an exhausted treasury without perpetuating the taxes, and the revenue shall be proportioned to the expenditures of the government and the exigencies of the times. The tariff produced nullification, and we should fear that either horn of the dilemma would produce a worse catastrophe than slavery, or an attempt at indemnity for abolition of it. Self-preservation is said to be the first law of nature, and I understand, as I think every other rational man will understand, self-preservation to mean as well the preservation of their property as their lives; and for this reason, too, we had better close with alternative.

Those matters, taken in connection with the present rate of taxes, will realize a sufficiency of funds under the direction of a wise legislature and prudent economy, to support the expenses of a respectable state government until our population and taxable property, as a state, will increase in a ration proportioned to our wants.

We have everything to hope from the liberality of the present administration, and as we hold the same rank in the scale of creation with our contemporaries of the states, let us have the same rights in Congress and exercise the manly prerogative of governing ourselves, as becomes the descendants of '76 old times.[2]

---

2 Ibid.

A State Government or Not? That Is the Question

The author of the few suggestions now offered to the public has been averse to a speedy change of our political condition. The taxes will be much increased, and the liberality of the national government lessened. Our governor and judges may not be as good as those sent us by Uncle Sam, nor will they, for many years, be as well paid. The objections on the score of present pecuniary interest and the want of a stable population, etc., are strong. The stop of many useful appropriations by Congress may be felt for a moment. These matters have weighed much with me against any application for admission into the Union for some years to come. But after all, there is not so much in these objections as many, on first blush, seem to imagine. We cannot expect to live and fatten forever on the proceeds of the national treasury; and the sooner we feel the necessity of shifting for ourselves, by industry and economy, the better. All cannot be fed at Uncle Sam's table. A favored few only can be admitted. Our taxes, if high, will fall on the property and wealth—will be expended here—and can neither ruin nor oppress the people. We shall have a stable or respectable community, so much to be desired, until we cease to be a mere providence or distant plantation of the empire. We must assume the rank of a state and exercise the privilege of self-government. The people are a sort of semislaves without self-government.

There is something humiliating and revolting to the pride and spirit of freemen to be ruled by officers sent from a distance. It is too much like the condition of the old British colonies, where every man had to cry aloud "God save the King." And a man, to have half a chance here for anything, must pull off his hat and say, "God bless the president, the governor, and perhaps the delegate, too." Indeed, the little governor, our secretary, will have to be blessed soon to enable a fellow to get along. Let us have governors and judges of our own choice. I should rather pay more taxes and have less money, to feel the pride and independence of a freeman. The substantial citizens of the states will not remove here so readily until we become a state and our lives, liberties, and property are places under the protection of the constitution, laws, and courts of the United States.

Both Michigan and Florida are pressing into the rank and society of the states and are ambitious to have two senators in Congress. The western states—our best friends in time of need—summon us to put on the state cockade and stand by them when we see other sections of the Union struggling for additional power and influence. Will Arkansas back out and refuse to aid her friends for fear of a little tax or that Uncle Sam will not milk so freely as before? No—she will shoulder her political firelock and fight with her western friends.

Another reason has influence with me. I like rotation in office, and especially in the Executive Department. In most of the states, the governor and secretary are only appointed for three or four years. It is against the principles of democracy for executive power to continue long in the same hands. We have had Pope and Fulton over us for five or six years, and I suppose we are to have them as much longer. Pope talks of giving up, but it is all talk. He will never quit, so long as he can keep down Crittenden and his party with the Ten Sections and the state house. As for Fulton, he hardly thinks his reign has commenced. More especially, if he should get a patent for his late discovery, a grant of all power to the governor is only half as much as a grant of all power to the legislature.

If Michigan and Florida are admitted into the Union and we are left behind, Arkansas will justly be considered the fag-end of the Republic—the black sheep of the American flock.

Fellow citizens of this territory, let me tell you that in the history of the world, no people ever attained glory or renown or were long free who were not characterized by a lofty pride and tone of distinction. I have now given a few hints on the question of going into a state government, without feeling a strong conviction of the policy or propriety of the measure. My mind is filled with doubt—indeed, I am rather inclined against it—but I have stated a few of the reasons for and against the step to awaken your attention to the subject. I expect you to examine the matter with coolness and candor and decide according to your honest opinion of the public interest, regardless of the opinions or wishes of any man or set of men. You may hear from me again.[3]

---

3 Ibid.

Chapter 3

<u>In the Union or Out of It?</u>

We copy the following from the *Helena Herald,* sixth edition. The editor, it will be seen, considers the reasons urged by Mr. Sevier for applying for our admission into the Union as a state entirely justifiable, though he firmly regrets their existence. He would prefer our remaining as a territory for a few years to come. This, we believe, is the opinion and wish of almost every reflecting man in the territory.

<u>State Government</u>

On March 16, 1834, we said "We are out of the United States!" This happy state of being, we are too well convinced, is not to be of long duration. The letter of the Hon. Ambrose H. Sevier shows that reasons entirely justifiable, though we truly regret their existence, have involved him in the necessity of presenting a "resolution—inquiring into the expediency of permitting the people of Arkansas to form a Constitution and come into the Union upon an equal footing with the original states."

To keep up a happy balance of power in the Senate of the United States is a matter of great importance, and indeed, we consider more likely than any other matter bringing the slave-holding states to an immediate sense of the danger that awaits them, should they permit the fanatics in the nonslaveholding states to get the ascendancy in the Senate. The day that such state of things is brought about, we may bid farewell to all the blessings of liberty, and vain will be our lamentations after fanaticism has taken our place and country. We had hoped to have enjoyed the inappreciable blessing of living out of the Union until the problem should have been dissolved, but such hope cannot be realized, and therefore, calm and serious discussion becomes every citizen of Arkansas.

We are to have a constitution and state government. What shall be the provisions, and what are the terms on which we will consent to come into the Union? These are grave questions and should have the most mature consideration before they are answered. Shall we have a southern independent state? Or shall we have a "free state," as one editor in the Territory has been pleased to express himself? He parries the repulse that might be expected to such an expression by saying that we are only "half free" in our present condition.

For our own part, if we come into the Union, there is nothing more certain than that we are for coming with all the blessings conferred by our fathers, as well as all the encumbrances with which slavery may be alleged, by the fanatics, to encumber us.

Let there be no dodging. Come out, every man. Are you for or against the measure? Will you have a "free state" in the sense understood by the fanatics and some deluded, designing, and illiberal citizens throughout the Union? Or will you have an independent state with the permission of hold or not holding slaves just as you think proper? We are for the latter, though we would prefer remaining as a Territory for some years to come if we could have had our wish.

Let us hear from you, readers, for we are decidedly for the popular voice being heard on this subject. Let us hear from every post office what the wishes of the people are. Good and generous readers, take into consideration the postage on your letters. We desire that we may not be taxed with it. It is the interest of us all to know the state of public feeling on this important question of "state or no state," and to tax the editor of a newspaper (the best channel for communication on all public matters), with the postage of letters containing an expression of public opinion, would be just as criminal as to dodge the question entirely.

Ready to Enter the Union

Mr. Editor, I fully concur in the opinion expressed by the honorary senator from Ohio (Mr. Ewing) as to the importance of the subject of our admission into the Union as an independent member of the Confederacy. It is of more importance to Arkansas than any event that will probably occur within the next half century. The proposed change from a territorial government into a state government has by common consent received the assent of the majority of the people.

The strongest objection urged against the adoption of a state government, on our part, is the expense attendant on the alteration of our relative situation. To this it may be answered that our population has increased, in number and resources, since the last census by at least one-fourth (probably more so in the south). By going into a state government, a large number of people would emigrate from the southern and western states immediately, and they will probably remain until after we get settled in our constitution and laws. Already indications from the south and west justify the belief that an unexampled tide of emigration will teem in upon us, occupy and cultivate the surplus lands, give a new impulse to agriculture and commerce, and create a temporary market at home for most articles of produce raised by our farmers. Owing to the sparse settlements in some of the countries, education has hitherto been too much neglected. As the population has increased, society must improve, and with it the necessity and means of keeping up common schools.

The general government has extended toward Arkansas a liberal hand in clearing out and removing obstructions to navigation, cutting and improving roads, etc. Some express a doubt, in the event of our admission into the Union, that the munificence of the parent government will be withdrawn. The government would possess the same right to the public domain that she now possesses, and any improvement in the navigation of a river, or construction of roads, would increase the value of the public lands in the vicinity of such road or water course. The government would be the principal gainer, and no doubt, it would pursue the same liberal policy that has heretofore characterized her course in relation to Arkansas.

Mr. Editor, it is now upward of fifty years since the close of the Revolutionary War, when the United States took their station among the independent powers of the civilized globe. New states have, from time to time, been admitted into the Union. Since that period their progress has been unexampled. There were but thirteen states in the Union when the war commenced, and there are now twenty-four. The population, which then amounted to two million and a half, is now upward of thirteen million. The principles of those harmonious and beautiful republican institutions, of which America is justly proud, are to be attributed to the free spirit of the people. The wisdom of American statesmen has developed these principles more fully, raised those institutions to a degree hitherto unexampled, and realized a system of polity more economical, orderly, rational, and conducive to human improvement, national prosperity, and happiness than any that has yet existed in the world. After a period of thirteen years, Arkansas finds her population sufficient to entitle her to a voice in the councils of the nation and her resources ample to meet the increased expenditure consequent on her elevation as a sovereign and independent member of this glorious Confederacy that has compelled the world to wonder.

As some changes must necessarily occur on our admission into the Union, I may, if you think them worthy of publication, offer a few numbers on the benefits of education and constitution and the advantages of our soil and climate over the less-favored portions of the Union.

Chapter 4

The Constitutional Convention

Convention Act

Section 1. Be it enacted, by the General Assembly of the Territory of Arkansas, that it shall and may be lawful for the qualified voters of each county in the territory to assemble at the several precincts or places of holding elections, heretofore established by law. It shall also be lawful in each township, of the several counties, to elect and choose representatives to form a constitution in convention for the people of said territory, preparatory to their admission into the Union as one of United States of America. Representatives or delegates to said convention shall be apportioned among the several counties as follows: from the county of Pulaski, including the counties of White and Saline, three representatives; from county of Hot Spring, one representative; from the county of Jefferson, one representative; from the county of Clark, one representative; from the of county Pike, one representative; from the county of Hempstead, two representatives; from the county of Lafayette, one representative; from the county of Miller, one representative; from the county of Sevier, one representative; from the county of Union, one representative; from the county of Mississippi, one representative; from the county of Crittenden, two representatives; from the county of St. Francis, two representatives; from the county of Phillips, two representatives; from the counties of Jefferson and Arkansas, one representative; from the county of Monroe, one representative; from the county of Chicot, two representatives; from the counties of Lawrence and Randolph, four representatives; from the county of Greene, one representative; from the county of Independence, two representatives; from the county of Jackson, one representative; from the counties of Izard and Carroll, one representative; from the county of Washington, six representatives; from the county of Crawford, three representatives; from the county of Scott, one representative; from the county of Johnson, one representative; from the counties of Pope and Johnson, one representative; from the county of Van Buren, one representative; and from the county of Conway, one representative.

And the election for said representatives shall be held on the second Monday in December next at the several precincts in the several townships throughout the several counties in the said territory, previous notice of which shall be given in a public manner, as required by law—in other cases by the sheriffs of the several counties, under the same penalties and liabilities as prescribed in other similar cases. The elections shall be held by the same judges and conducted in the same manner and under the same regulations, as prescribed by the laws of said territory regulating elections therein for members of the General Assembly of said territory. The polls shall be opened and compared, and the elections certified in the same manner.

Section 2. And be it further enacted that the members of the convention, thus duly elected, are hereby authorized to meet in the town of Little Rock on the first Monday in January next; and before they proceed to the discharge of their duties, they shall be sworn by some officer legally authorized to administer an oath to support the Constitution of the United States of America and the best interests of the whole people of Arkansas. The convention, when met, shall first determine by a majority of the whole number elected whether or not it be expedient at that time to form a constitution and state government, provided the same shall be republican and not inconsistent with or repugnant to the constitution of the United States.

Section 3. And be it further enacted that in case the said convention shall form a constitution and state government for the people of the Territory of Arkansas, the said convention, as soon thereafter as may be, shall cause a true copy of said constitution or frame of government to be transmitted to Congress for its approbation. When approved of by

Congress, and Arkansas is admitted into the Union as a state according to the principles of the Federal Constitution, the constitution shall be the supreme law of the state of Arkansas.

Section 4. And be it further enacted that said convention shall be the judge of the qualification and election of its own members; shall make its own officers, regulations, and bylaws; and shall have power to preserve order and to imprison for contempt for any period not beyond the end of the sessions. Each member shall receive the sum of two dollars per day during his attendance in said convention, and two dollars for every twenty-five miles travel in going to and returning from the place of holding said convention, and the services and compensation of the members of said convention shall be certified by the president of the said convention and countersigned by its secretary. Certificates shall be sufficient vouchers to the auditor of the territory, who, upon such certificates being presented, is hereby required to issue warrants for the several amounts to the respective members, directed to the treasurer of the territory, who is hereby required to pay the same as other debts.

Section 5. And be it further enacted that all the necessary expenses of said convention—stationery, fuel, house rent, or any other convenience necessary to the comfort of said convention, or the progression of its business—for a secretary, doorkeeper, or other necessary officers of said convention shall be paid out of the Territorial Treasury; and the certificate of the president of said convention, countersigned by its secretary, shall be a sufficient voucher to the auditor for the whole or any part thereof. Upon presentation of such a certificate or certificates to him, he is hereby required to issue warrants directed to the treasurer, who is hereby required and directed to pay the same as other debts.

Convention Bill Adopted

The Convention Bill provides that delegates shall be elected on December 14, 1835, and convene at Little Rock on January 4, 1836.

Monday, October 19, 1835, General Assembly House of Representatives

Mr. Fowler, from the Joint Committee, to which was referred so much of the governor's message as relates to the state government, reported a bill to be entitled an act for the election of members to a convention to form a constitution and system of government for the people of Arkansas, preparatory to their admission into the Union as a state. Mr. Whinnery moved to dispense with the rules of the house in order to read said bill a second time, which was negative. Mr. Walker of Hempstead offered the following amendment to the bill: "strike out all that part apportioning the representation from the various counties, and introduce in lieu thereof that the representation in the convention shall be the same as that in the present legislature, including members of both houses, and they shall be elected in the same manner as they now are." The bill was read a first time and passed to a second reading.

———————

Tuesday, October 20, 1835, House of Representatives

A bill to be entitled an act for the election of members to a convention to form a constitution and system of government for the people of Arkansas, preparatory to their admission into the Union as a state was read a second time. Mr. Walker of Hempstead moved the following amendment which was read a first time. Mr. Walker of Hempstead moved to dispense with the rules of the House in order to read the amendment a second time. The question being on the amendment, Mr. Walker of Hempstead called for the yeas and nays which were as follows: yeas, 18; nays, 15. And so the amendment was adopted (to change the basis of representation).

On the motion of Mr. Walker of Hempstead, the house resolved itself into a Committee of the Whole on the bill, Mr. Hill in the chair, and after some time spent therein, the committee rose and reported the bill without amendment. Mr. Walker of Washington moved to recommit the bill to select a committee, with instructions to report a clause therein, giving to every five hundred free white male inhabitants the right to send one representative to said convention. Yeas and nays being called for by Mr. Fowler, the yeas and nays were as follows: yeas, 16; nays, 17. And so the motion was lost. The bill was then ordered to be engrossed for a third reading tomorrow.

———

Wednesday, October 21, 1835, House of Representatives

Mr. Fowler moved to reconsider a vote given by him on the order to engross the bill to be entitled an act for the election of members to a convention to form a constitution and system of government for the people of Arkansas, etc. Mr. Walker of Hempstead called for the yeas and nays on the motion, which were as follows: yeas, 19; nays, 14. And so the vote was reconsidered. Mr. Howell moved to reconsider the vote given by him yesterday on the motion of Mr. Walker of Washington, to commit the bill to a select committee, etc. The yeas and nays on the motion were called for and stood as on the last mentioned motion.

Mr. Walker of Washington then moved to recommit the bill to a select committee, with instructions to report a clause therein, giving to every five hundred free white males the right of electing a delegate to the convention, provided that each county should have one delegate. On this motion, Mr. Walker of Hempstead called for the yeas and nays, which were as follows: yeas, 17; nays, 16. So the bill was carried, and Messrs. Walker of Washington, Walker of Hempstead, Cummins, Logan, and Mathers appointed the select committee.

———

Thursday, October 22, 1835, House of Representatives

Mr. Walker of Washington reported the bill for forming a convention, with an amendment as instructed on yesterday. On the motion made to agree to the amendment, Mr. Walker of Hempstead called for the yeas and nays, which stood as follows: yeas, Messrs. Dunn, Evans, Fowler, Howell, Henderson, Jarrett, Logan, Mathers, Morton, Moore, Mangness, Porter, Stallings, Tennant, Walker of Washington, Ward, and Whinnery, 17; nays, Messrs. Bowie, Cummins, Ellis, Hill, Holman, Lee, Outlaw, Peal, Roberts, Seay, Shae, Scruggs, Triplett, Troy, Walker of Hempstead, and Mr. Speaker, 16.

So the report was agreed to. Mr. Whinnery moved that the rules of the House be dispensed with and the bill read a third time, which was done. Mr. Walker of Hempstead moved to amend by striking out the word two (as the per diem pay of members) and inserting five, which was negative, and the bill was read the third time. Mr. Cummins offered an amendment, giving every county one member and then dividing the whole number of free white males into the divisions of five hundred and giving each division one member. Before the vote could be taken on the amendment, the House adjourned.

————

Friday, October 23, 1835, Legislative Council

The bill, from the House of Representatives, entitled, "An act for the election of members to a convention to form a constitution and system of government for the people of Arkansas, preparatory to their admission into the Union as a state," was taken up and twice read, when Mr. Moore offered an amendment to the bill, changing the system of representation in the convention, which was rejected by the council, by yeas and nays, as follows: yeas, 14; nays, 14.

Mr. Thornton then moved to lay the bill on the table until the first day of January next, which was decided in the negative as follows: yeas, 5; nays, 23.

Mr. Clark of Chicot then moved to commit the bill to a Committee of the Whole, which was decided in the affirmative, as follows: yeas, 16; nays, 12.

House of Representatives

On the motion of Mr. Walker of Washington, the House took up the order of the day, Mr. Whinnery in the chair, which was the bill to elect members to a convention for forming a state constitution. Mr. Wilson offered amendment to the amendment of Mr. Cummins offered yesterday, which was lost. Mr. Mathers moved the previous question, and Mr. Cummins withdrew his amendment. The question being on the final passage of the bill, the yeas and nays were called for and stood as follows: yeas, Messrs. Bowie, Cummins, Dunn, Ellis, Evans, Fowler, Howell, Hill, Henderson, Holman, Jarrett, Lee, Logan, Mathers, Morton, Moore, Mangness, Porter, Peel, Seay, Stallings, Scruggs, Tennant, Walker of Washington, Ward, and Mr. Speaker, 26; nays, Messrs. Outlaw, Roberts, Shaw, Triplet, Troy, Walker of Hempstead, and Wilson, 7. And so the billed passed.

Saturday, October 24, 1835, Legislative Council

On the motion of Mr. Bean, the council resolved itself into a Committee of the Whole, Mr. Wolf in the chair, on the Convention Bill; and after spending some time in the consideration thereof, the committee rose and reported the bill, with an amendment which was concurred in by the council, as follows: yeas, 15; nays, 13.

The bill was then read a third time, and on the question of the passing of the bill, the yeas and nays were required, and were as follows: yeas, Messrs. Buzzard, Bradley, Clark of Chicot, Izard, Kelly, Lattimore, Mills, Moore, McKean, Ringgold, Smith, Taylor, Tidwell, Whittington, Williamson, Young, and Mr. President, 17; nays, Messrs. Bean, Brown, Clark of Carroll, Croft, Judkins, Kuykendall, Lafferty, Patrick, Pitman, Thornton, and Wolf, 11. So the bill passed and was sent to the House of Representatives for concurrence in the amendment.

House of Representatives

A message was received from the council announcing the passage of the bill that originated in this house, for the election of delegates to a convention to form a state constitution with amendments, which was passed to a second reading.

———————

Monday, October 26, 1835, Legislative Council

The Convention Bill was then taken up, as amended and returned by the House of Representatives, and the amendments being read, Mr. Smith proposed to amend the bill so as to give Arkansas County two members, which was negative. Mr. Thornton then moved to amend it so as to reduce the number of members in the convention to forty-two, which was also negative, by yeas and nays as follows: yeas, 5; nays, 24.

The question then occurred upon the amendment from the House of Representatives, which was decided by yeas and nays, as follows: yeas, 25; nays, 4. So the amendment was concurred in by the council.

———————

Monday, October 26, 1835, House of Representatives

The bill to elect members to a convention, etc., was taken up when Mr. Walker of Washington offered an amendment to the amendment made by the council; and the question being on agreeing to the amendment, the yeas and nays were called for and were as follows: yeas, 27; nays, 6. So the amendment to the amendment made by the council was adopted, and the bill returned to the council for concurrence therein.

———————

Tuesday, October 27, 1835, General Assembly: House of Representatives

A message was received from the council concerning the passage of the Convention Bill with the amendment.

Wednesday, October 28, 1835, House of Representatives

The Committee on Enrollments reported the following bills as correctly enrolled: an act calling a convention for forming a constitution preparatory to the admission of Arkansas into the Union.

List of Acts

Passed at the ninth session of the General Assembly of the Territory of Arkansas, to call a convention to form a constitution, etc.

Counter Report Made

The minority of the Joint Committee held it to be unnecessary, impolite, and inexpedient for the General Assembly to legislate on the subject of a state government at this time.

October 27, 1835

The following counter report was made in the House of Representatives on the fourteenth by Mr. Walker of Hempstead County, from the minority of the committee on the subject of state government.

The minority of the Joint Committee, to whom was referred that portion of the governor's message relating to a state government, have had the same under consideration and would respectfully report the following:

The minority of said committee do heartily concur in the opinions of His Excellency the Governor, so far as they are expressed in his message to this legislature and explained in the publications heretofore that lay before the public over the signature of His Excellency. The minority deem it unnecessary to recapitulate the arguments which have been already exhibited to the public on this subject, but would state that it is considered by said minority that the present action of this legislature on the subject of the admission of Arkansas into the Union, further than by memorial to Congress, is unnecessary, impolite, and illegal. As it regards the necessity of action on this case at the present time, it has been contended that the citizens of this territory do not enjoy the rights and privileges of American citizens and are in a state of vassalage and dependence. Therefore it is necessary that we throw off the chains and assert our freedom and independence. From this the minority would dissent, and would contend, that the citizens of this territory are free and have always been free, and that so for being in a state of slavery or dependence, their privileges and immunities are greater than those of many of the states who are now living under constitutions of their own formation. That the organic law of this territory, which is, to all intents and purposes, the constitution of the land, is purely republican and secures to every citizen all the rights and privileges of free American citizens, except in so far as the elections of governor, secretary, and judges are concerned. Again it has been urged that should Michigan be admitted into the Union previous to the admission of Arkansas, that the balance now existing between the slave and nonslaveholding states would be destroyed, and Arkansas, as a slave state, will be forever excluded. This question the minority consider has been already decided, and when the Congress of the United States in their wisdom determined on the Missouri questions that no new state tolerating slavery should be admitted north of the latitude of 36 degrees, it was saying to the whole world that all new states south of this latitude should be permitted to determine this point for themselves.

The minority would contend that the measure is impolite from the consideration of the embarrassed finances of the territory. Heretofore the general government has made liberal appropriations for the support of the territory; and the salaries of our governor, secretary, and judges, and also the compensation to the members of the legislature, including incidental expenses, have all been paid from the coffers of the general government. Yet our fiscal concerns are in a ruinous situation and our treasury insolvent. And though our taxes are high, yea, higher than in almost any portion of the Union, yet are we unable to meet the ordinary expenses of territorial government. What then would be our situation were our expenses increased, as they necessarily must be, should we push ourselves hastily into a state government? The impolicy of the measure is further urged from the consideration of the absolute inability of the territory to carry on and complete the necessary opening of rivers and constructing of roads, which is so necessary for the well-being of the citizens of this territory. Heretofore the general government has dealt out, with a liberal hand, the treasures of the nation for the purposes and already have many important roads been constructed through the liberality of Congress, which now are, through the poverty of the territory, going rapidly to decay. Many important roads keep up the necessary communication between the different parts of the territory, and which, if the liberality of Congress were restrained, must remain unopened perhaps forever. The impolicy of the measure is further urged from the inability of the citizens of the territory to defend themselves from the aggression of their enemies. Surrounded as we are by numerous powerful and uncivilized tribes of savages, with an unorganized and unarmed militia, the minority are of opinion (though they have a most exalted opinion of the chivalry and bravery of the hardy pioneers of Arkansas) that our frontier would be in an exposed and dangerous situation were the president to withdraw the national troops now established on our borders, and this might be expected were this measure adopted.

The illegality of the measure is urged from the want of authority on the part of this legislature to act in the manner proposed. Acting under the organic law, it has become our only authority. It is, to all intents and purposes, our sole and only constitution, and the minority can find no clause of that document which either directly or indirectly justifies or permits the calling of a convention by this honorable body. 'Tis true that the Constitution of the United States says "that new States may be admitted in the Union;" but your minority would ask if this justifies what might be called a forcible entry.

The illegality is further urged from the consideration that Congress has the right and power in themselves to designate and point out the bounds of every new state and previous admission. The course recommended by the resolution of the majority of this committee, if adopted, will virtually take this right from the general government and appropriate it to the convention.

The illegality of the measure is urged, for the consideration of the territory has not a population entitling it to representation in Congress under the present ratio of representation. From the late returns, the territory contains forty-eight thousand, nearly, in federal population. Now if we strike off from this aggregate that portion of population which lies south of the Red River, and which is evidently included in Texas, will be reduced to a fraction below that which would entitle us to representation. True it is, the government has extended her jurisdiction over this country, but it is supposed by all parties that when the line is run the whole, or at least a large portion of this territory, will be taken from Arkansas. All is respectfully submitted, and the following resolution presented: it is resolved, that it is unnecessary, impolite, and inexpedient to legislate on the subject of a state government at this time.

Apportionment for the Constitutional Convention

November 3, 1835
The Convention Bill

As published in our paper, the bill has become a law—but without the signature of the governor. He yesterday returned it to the House of Representatives, without either his approval or veto, but with a letter explaining his reasons for not taking any part in it, either in approving or disapproving the step. Having retained it in his possession over three days, it becomes a law without any action on it on his part. If we can procure a copy, we will publish his letter in our next paper, together with some other papers on the subject which he transmitted to the legislature at the same time.

The legislature, we believe, have made no provision for promulgating the Convention Bill among the people, other than its publication in pamphlet form, with the other laws, which cannot be published in time for circulation before the election of delegates, which takes place on the second Monday of December next (fourteenth next month). It may, therefore, not be amiss for us to publish below, for general information and for easy reference, a list of the counties with the number of delegates to the convention apportioned to each.

Counties	Number of Delegates
Pulaski, including White and Saline	3
Hot Spring	1
Jefferson	1
Clark	1
Pike	1
Hempstead	2
Lafayette	1
Miller	1
Sevier	1
Miller and Sevier, jointly	1
Union	1
Mississippi	1
Crittenden	2
St. Francis	2
Phillips	2
Arkansas	1
Jefferson and Arkansas, jointly	1
Monroe	1

Chicot	2
Lawrence and Randolph, jointly	4
Greene	1
Independence	2
Jackson	1
Izard	1
Carroll	1
Izard and Carroll, jointly	1
Washington	6
Crawford	3
Scott	1
Pope	1
Johnson	1
Pope and Johnson, jointly	1
Van Buren	1
Conway	1
Total	52

The meeting of the Convention is to take place on the first Monday of January next (fourth day), for the purpose of forming a constitution for the future state of Arkansas, and the compensation to the delegates is fixed at two dollars per day.

Governor Fulton's Statement on the Statehood Bill

November 10, 1835
The Governor's Message and the Opinion of the Attorney General

Gentleman of the House of Representatives:

I regret that I could not approve the bill which originated in your House, and which was delivered to me some days since, providing for the election of members to a convention to form a constitution and system of government for the people of Arkansas, preparatory to their admission into the Union as a state. My reasons for withholding my approval were because I did believe the general assembly of the Territory of Arkansas possessed the power to pass such an act, and that, as the executive officer of a territorial government erected by acts of Congress, I had no power to sanction or concur in such an act.

I deem it needless to repeat the arguments which I have heretofore used in support of my views upon this question. The people have differed from me in opinion upon it and instructed their representatives to pass the bill for the formation of state constitution. Although I cannot approve this act, yet I am determined to do everything in my power, I have calculated to enable the people to meet in primary assemblies in a peaceable manner in order to petition Congress for a change of government.

Both branches of the legislature having passed the bill by such large majorities, as clearly to indicate that it would have passed a second time in each house by a majority of more than two-thirds, I have considered it useless to return the bill to you with objections for reconsideration. Agreeably, therefore, to the provision of the organic law, the bill has now become an act without my signature, so far as it is consistent with the constitution and laws of the United States establishing a territorial government in Arkansas.

My abiding faith in the people of Arkansas, in sustaining the laws of their country, is such that I entertain no fears of an attempt on their part to interfere with the existing government or interrupt the territorial officers in the regular discharge of their duties, until they have obtained the authority of Congress to abrogate and change the territorial government and erect in its stead a state government. I am confident of being able to maintain, in the meantime, the supremacy of the laws of the United States in the government of this territory.

I herewith send you a copy of the opinion of the attorney general of the United States upon the important constitutional and legal questions involved in the measure received a few days since, and which has been transmitted to me by the authority of the president for my guidance. I respectfully request that it may be printed and circulated under the authority of the legislature for the information of the people and direct them in making the change of government which they now have in contemplation.

WM. S. FULTON, November 2, 1835

Work of the Legislature

October 27, 1835

The Convention Bill has passed both houses of the legislature and now only wants the signature of approval within three days to become a law. We are not advised as to the course which he will purse in relation to the bill, but we are informed that it is pretty certain that he will not veto it. If this information be correct, we may now congratulate our fellow citizens on the settlements of this much agitated question, and on the flattering prospect which it opens to us of speedily becoming one of the states of the American Confederacy.

We have procured a copy of the bill—it finally passed—which we have the pleasure of presenting to our readers in another column, and we think it will be found to give general satisfaction to the people. The best evidence of this is that fact that neither the northern or southern members seem to be entirely satisfied with it. Our impression is that the representation in the convention is fixed on an equitable basis, and that neither party has cause either to triumph or complain.

For the purpose of preventing the further spread of an erroneous impression, which seems to prevail to some extent with respect to the cause of the difference between the two contending parties in the legislature in relation to fixing the basis of representation in the convention, we have obtained from a gentleman, who was present in the House of

Representatives during the whole discussion, the following brief outline of the arguments used by some of the speakers on the much vexed question.

Both houses of the legislature have been occupied during the past week in discussing the proper representation in the convention. The report of the Joint Committee—curtailing the representation of the people as now represented in the two houses—was not satisfactory to most of the members. It was accordingly disagreed to by the House of Representatives (as stated in our last) when a motion, made by Mr. Walker of Hempstead (who, although at first unfriendly to the formation of a state government at this time, ceased his opposition to the details of the bill when he found it useless to persist—a large majority being decidedly in favor of the main question), was agreed to by the House, giving the same representation in the convention that now constitutes both houses of the legislature. By this proposition, each county was allowed one member as a representative of the county, and then every five hundred white males, according to the governor's apportionment of the members of the present House of Representatives, was to be entitled to one representative. This amendment was opposed by Mr. Walker of Washington and Fowler Pulaski and sustained by the mover and by Mr. Cummins of Pulaski, who urged that it gave to the several counties of the territory one representative at least and one additional representative, according to the white male population. He said he was in favor of the measure, principally because by giving each county one, as a district representation, it would create a balance of power and check the sectional feelings, which had unfortunately sprung up in the legislature and which would most probably be imparted to the people and again influence the convention in forming the Constitution. He urged that since sectional interest seemed to exist in the territory, it was the duty of the legislature to guard against their having any improper influence by giving a district representation, which was the mode adopted in the formation of the Federal Constitution, to balance and unite the different districts. By destroying the representation of the counties in the convention and assuming any other basis, the district or county interests would most probably be neglected, or at least it would place the rights of the less populous counties in the hands of the more populous and enable a small district to entirely destroy the rights of small counties because it was most populous. One-fourth or one-eighth of the whole territory might, according to any other principle, govern all the balance. This would not be justice, would not be Republican in principle, and would really be tyranny, that a small district shall govern the whole because it happened at the moment to be the most populous.

On the House agreeing to this amendment, Mr. Walker of Washington moved to refer the bill to a select committee, with instructions to so amend it that each five hundred white males should be the basis for electing one representative to the convention. This was opposed by Messrs. Walker of Hempstead and Cummins on the grounds that it destroyed the county representation and gave the entire control of the destinies of the country to a few of the populous counties. The motion was lost.

The next morning reconsideration was called for and carried by one vote. Mr. Walker of Washington then moved an amendment that each five hundred white males should afford the basis for representative in the convention, and providing that, where a county contained less than five hundred white males, should have one representative. This amendment, after a long and animated debate, was at length adopted by a majority of one vote in the House of Representatives, and the amendment was concurred with by the Council.

April 26, 1836, Arkansas's Delegate from Washington City

This is an extract of a letter from a highly respectable citizen of Arkansas on a visit of private business to Washington City to a gentleman of this place.

Washington, March 27, 1836

Our friend Col. Sevier seems to be a general favorite, and I have not yet heard the first unkind or disrespectful sentiment expressed toward him. On the contrary, I have heard many persons say (and my own observation induces me to concur in it) that there is no one belonging to the house of which he is a member who commands more influence with the departments, or is more efficient. I have found him continually at his post and exemplary in his habits. He entertains no fears about the eventual success of the application for admission. Tomorrow is the day fixed upon for taking up the bill in both houses, not however, for final action; but I presume all the objections will be elicited and subsequent debate dispensed with if we succeed.

Chapter 5

The Constitutional Convention Meets

January 5, 1836, Meeting of the Convention

Yesterday being the day appointed for the meeting of the convention to form a constitution for the future state of Arkansas, the members who had arrived met at the Baptist Meeting house at twelve o'clock and proceeded temporarily to organize by calling Mark Bean Esq., of Washington County, to the chair and appointing John Hutt, Esq., of Little Rock, secretary pro tem.

The members present were then called upon by counties to produce their credentials, which was accordingly done, when they were qualified and took their seats. It appeared that no members answered from the counties of Mississippi, Greene, and Miller and Sevier, and that one member from Crittenden was still absent. Judge Roane of Jefferson moved an adjournment until this morning to give the absent members time to arrive; and the question being taken, it was decided in the affirmative and the Convention adjourned to this morning at ten o'clock.

It is understood that Judge Ellis, the member elected from Miller and Sevier, was too much indisposed to attend and that he may not be expected during the session.

———

This morning at ten o'clock, the convention again met, according to adjournment, when the president pro tem, having taken the chair, and the members from Greene and the absent member from Crittenden having appeared, qualified, and taken their places. The roll was called, and the following members answered to their names.

Arkansas—Bushrod W. Lee

Carroll—John F. King

Clark—John Wilson

Conway—Nimrod Menefee

Crawford—James Woodson Bates

Richard—C. S. Brown, John Drennen

Chicot—John Clark and A. H. Davis

Crittenden—John W. Calvert and Wright W. Elliott

Greene—G. I. Martin

Hot Spring—James S. Conway

Hempstead—Grandson D. Royston and James H. Walker

Independence—Townsend Dickinson and John Ringgold

Izard—Charles Sanders

Izard and Carroll—John Adams

Jackson—John Robinson

Jefferson—Sam C. Roane

Jefferson and Arkansas—Terence Farrelly

Johnson—Lorenzo N. Clarke

Lafayette—Josiah N. Wilson

Lawrence and Randolph—David W. Lowe, Robert Smith, Thomas S. Drew, and Henry Slavens

Miller—Travis G. Wright

Monroe—Thomas W. Lacy

Pulaski, White and Saline—John McLain, Wm. Cummins, and Absalom Fowler

Phillips—Henry L. Bisco and George W. Ferabee

Pike—Elijah Kelly

Pope—Thomas Murray

Pope and Johnson—Andrew Scott

Scott—Silver Marshall

Sevier—Joseph W. McKean

St. Francis—Wm. Strong and Caleb S. Manly

Union—Andrew J May

Van Buren—Walker W. Trimble

Washington—David Walker, Mark Bean, Wm. Mock, Ball, Robert McCamy, A. Whinnery, James Moon

The convention then proceeded to the election, by ballot, of a president. Mr. Drew nominated John Ringgold, Mr. Scott nominated James Woodson Bates, and Mr. Conway nominated John Wilson. Messrs. Conway and Boon were appointed tellers and proceeded to receive the ballots, and on counting the same, the votes appeared as:

John Wilson	24 votes
John Ringgold	16 votes
J. W. Bates	9 votes
R. McKay	1 vote

And appearing that no one had a majority of the whole number of ballots, a second ballot was resorted to, which resulted as follows:

John Wilson	28 votes
John Ringgold	22 votes

Whereupon, John Wilson of Clark County, having a majority of the whole number of votes, was declared duly elected president of the convention, and he was accordingly conducted to the chair and proceeded to the discharge of the duties of that office.

The convention then proceeded to ballot for secretary, and Charles P. Bertrand and John Hutt were nominated and the ballots received and counted. The election resulted as follows:

Charles P. Bertrand	32 votes
John Hutt	18 votes

Whereupon, Charles P. Bertrand, having received a majority of the whole number of ballots, was declared duly elected secretary of the convention and accordingly took the usual oath and proceeded to the discharge of the duties of the office.

The convention then proceeded to ballot for a doorkeeper, which election resulted as follows:

Asa G. Baker	34 votes
James V. Patton	16 votes

Whereupon, Asa G. Baker having received a majority of the whole number of votes, was declared duly elected doorkeeper and sergeant at arms of the convention, and after taking the usual oath, he proceeded to the discharge of his duties.

A resolution was offered by Mr. Roane that it be expedient for this convention to proceed to form a constitution and state government, which was adopted with only one dissenting vote (from Mr. Walker of Hempstead).

On motion of Mr. Farrelly, the president was authorized to appoint the following standing committees: executive, to consist of seven members; judiciary, to consist of nine members; legislative, to consist of eleven members; and revenue, to consist of nine members.

Only one member (who is expected) was absent at the meeting of the convention this morning: Mr. Ross of Mississippi County, who has not yet arrived but who is hourly looked for.

We shall endeavor, as usual on such occasions, to furnish our readers with as full a report of the proceedings of the convention as our limits will admit of.

The Constitutional Convention met in the Baptist meeting house for the first few days. It then met in the Presbyterian church, which stood near the corner of Main and Second (then Cherry) Streets. The committee appointed to provide a suitable house for the accommodation of the convention reported that it could find no building "that affords so many facilities, and comforts as the Presbyterian church, which has been tendered to your committee at $100 in territorial script." It was thereupon resolved by the convention that the proposals of the trustees of the Presbyterian church be accepted.

Standing Committees of Constitutional Convention

January 12, 1836, Journal of Convention

Mr. Walker of Hempstead, from the committee appointed to draft rules for the convention, during the session reported sundry rules that were read and adopted.

On the motion of Mr. Walker of Washington, a committee of seven was ordered to be appointed to prepare and report a Declaration of Rights for the inhabitants of the future state of Arkansas.

Thursday, January 7, 1836

The president announced the appointment of the following standing committees.

Executive: Messrs. Conway, Roane, Whinnery, Ball, Murray, Smith, and Walker of Hempstead
Judiciary: Messrs. Scott, Royston, Dickinson, Adams, Fowler, Biscoe, Marshall, McCamy, and Drew
Legislative: Messrs. Bates, Lacy, McKean, Bean, Clark of Chicot, Ringgold, Farrelly, Lafferty, Sanders, King and Cummins
Revenue: Messrs. David, McLain, Walker of Washington, Robinson, Calvert, Strong, Clarke of Johnson, May, and Wilson of Layette
Boundaries: Messrs. Brown, Boon, Drennen, Wright, Strong, Kelly, and Menefee
To draft the Bill of Rights: Messrs. Walker of Washington, Lee, Ferebee, Low, Martin, Slavens, and Royston
To deal with miscellaneous subjects: Messrs. Manly, McCamy, Elliot, Davis, Bean, May, and Martin

To prepare an ordinance or compact: Messrs. Ball, Roane, Kelly, Biscoe, and Brown

(Subsequent reports by these committees during the following days were finally incorporated in the state constitution.)

Friday, January 1836

On the motion of Mr. Fowler, a standing committee on the militia was ordered to be appointed. On the motion of Mr. Marshall, a committee was ordered to draft a schedule to the Constitution. On the motion of Mr. Ball, the committee on the judiciary was instructed to inquire into the expediency of abolishing imprisonment for debt within the state of Arkansas.

Saturday, January 9, 1836

The president announced the appointment of the following committees.

To draft a schedule to the Constitution: Messrs. Marshall, Walker of Hempstead, Lacy, Dickinson, Biscoe, McCamy, McLain, Wilson of Lafayette, and Drew

To deal with the militia: Messrs. Fowlers, McKean, Clark of Chicot, Ringgold, and Whinnery

Monday, January 11, 1836

Mr. Walker of Washington, from the committee to draft the Bill of Rights, submitted a report on the subject which was laid on the table and ordered to be printed.

Reports of Committees Made to the Convention

Tuesday, January 12, 1836, Journal of Convention

Mr. Scott, from the committee on the judiciary, made the following report.

The standing committee on the judiciary, which has been instructed to inquire the expediency of abolishing imprisonment for debt, according to order, have had the same under consideration and gone through the subject. They ask leave to report that they deem it inexpedient for this convention, in forming a fundamental law of the land, either wholly to abolish imprisonment for debt or to leave the subject entirely open for future action. It is the opinion of your committee that, without fraud on the part of the debtor, he should not be incarcerated after he had made a surrender of his estate for the benefit of his creditors. To say that no debtor should be imprisoned, whether his conduct was influenced by honesty or fraud, would be leaving a door too wide open for the crafty and unprincipled. They, therefore, recommend the insertion of a clause in the Bill of Rights of the state of Arkansas to the effect of the following and ask to be discharged from the further consideration of the subject: the person of a debtor, except when there is strong presumption of fraud, shall neither be imprisoned nor continue in prison after delivering up his estate for the benefit of his creditors in such manner as may be prescribed by law.

Laid on the table and ordered printed.

Wednesday, January 13, 1836

On the motion of Mr. Murray, a committee was ordered to take into consideration the subject of banking. Messrs. Murray, Davis, Roane, Biscoe, and McCamy were appointed to said committee.

The following resolution was offered by Mr. Fowler, and rejected: that the standing committee on the Legislative Department be instructed to inquire into the expediency of locating, permanently, the seat of the state government at Little Rock.

Tuesday, January 14, 1836

Mr. Calvert offered the following resolution, which lay on the table: that a committee be appointed to consist of eleven members to take into consideration the propriety of permanently locating the seat of government of the state of Arkansas at some convenient point on the Mississippi River.

Friday, January 15, 1836

This day was principally consumed in deciding questions of order and in offering and rejecting amendments to the report of the Executive Committee.

Saturday, January 16, 1836

Mr. Martin offered the following resolution which was rejected: that the president appoint a committee to consist of nine members to take under consideration the subject of instituting a Medical Board.

Monday, January 18, 1836

The report of the committee on boundaries and the report of the committee to draft a Declaration of Rights were considered in the Committee of the Whole; and the former was reported without amendments, and the latter with amendments. Both were laid on the table.

(Tuesday, January 19, 1836, was devoted to discussion of the report of the Legislative Committee and the adoption and rejection of various amendments to the report.)

Wednesday, January 20, 1836

On the motion of Mr. McCamy, the report of the committee on the judiciary, as amended, was recommitted to the same committee to revise and consolidate the same, and report thereon.

Thursday, January 21, 1836

Mr. Walker of Hempstead presented the credentials of George Halbrook, the member elect from Sevier and Miller Counties, in the room, for Richard Ellis resigned. Mr. Halbrook came forward, was qualified, and took his seat.

Mr. Scott from the committee on the judiciary, to whom the report of said committee, as amended, was recommitted, moved to be discharged from the further consideration of the subject, which was agreed to. The report was ordered to engross.

The report of the committee on banking was taken up, and amendments were offered by Mr. Bean, Mr. Farrelly, and Mr. Ringgold, which were all rejected. The report was laid on the table.

Friday, January 22, 1836

On the motion of Mr. Walker of Hempstead, a committee of three was ordered to be appointed to arrange article and the section, the various reports as they are engrossed, for the final action of the convention.

Saturday, January 23, 1836

The engrossed report on boundaries was taken up when Mr. Brown proposed an amendment that was lost when, on motion of the Mr. Scott, the report as engrossed was agreed to.

Monday, January 25, 1836

Mr. Fowler renewed his motion to refer the report (of the Legislative Committee) together with the amendments to a select committee, which was agreed to. Messrs. Fowler, Clark of C., Clark of J., McKean, and Drew were appointed to said committee.

———

February 2, 1836, Journal of Convention

Mr. Fowler, from the committee that was referred the report of the Legislative Committee, with the proposed amendments, made the following report: Mr. Murray moved the two members be appointed to wait on Judge Bates (who was unable to attend from indisposition) and receive his vote on the preceding report, which was agreed to.

The question was then taken on agreeing to the report of the select committee; and the yeas and nays being required were as follows: yeas, 28; nays, 22. So the report was agreed to.

On motion of Mr. Fowler, the thirty-third, thirty-fourth, thirty-fifth, and thirty-seventh sections of the original report were stricken out.

Mr. Bean moved to amend the thirtieth section which was negative by yeas and nays as follows: yeas, 23; nays, 23. The report was then on the motion of Mr. Walker of Hempstead ordered to be engrossed.

Wednesday, January 27, 1836

On the motion of Mr. Roane, a committee of five was ordered to be appointed to draft an address to the Congress of the United States to accompany the Constitution of the state of Arkansas; and Messrs. Roane, Ball, Conway, Cummins, and Biscoe were appointed to said committee.

Thursday, January 28, 1836

On the motion of Mr. Drennen, it was resolved that this convention will proceed tomorrow at three o'clock to elect by ballot a messenger to carry the Constitution of the state of Arkansas to Washington City.

Constitution Adopted and Arkansas Asks Admission

Friday, January 29, 1836

Mr. Roane, from the committee appointed to draft an address to Congress to accompany the Constitution, submitted the following report, which was adopted:

To the Senate and the House of Representatives in Congress assembled:

The people of Arkansas, through their representatives in convention assembled, respectfully represent to your honorable body that the Territory of Arkansas, by an accession of population within her limits, has now that number of inhabitants that justifies her to look with confidence to her admission into the Union, as one of the free and independent states of the American Confederacy, at as early a period as the necessary forms of admission can be complied with.

The people of Arkansas, animated with a desire for the enjoyment of independence and self-government, have, by an expression of their will, approximating to unanimity, elected representatives to meet in convention at the city of Little Rock, with full and ample powers to make a constitution and system of state government for Arkansas. The accompanying Constitution is the result of their deliberations.

Relying with entire confidence on the liberal policy of the United States that whatever will minister to the happiness, security, and interest of Arkansas will meet with a cordial and liberal response from the Congress of the United States, we respectfully ask your honorable body that Arkansas may be admitted on an equal footing with the original states in the Union at as early a period as practicable.

The report was adopted.

———————

Mr. Walker of Hempstead submitted the following resolution which was adopted: that the secretary is requested to make out two copies of the Constitution—one on parchment, the other on paper— one which shall be submitted to Congress, and the other shall be laid up in the archives of the state, for which service he shall be allowed one hundred dollars.

———————

On the motion of Mr. Strong, the convention then proceeded to the election of a messenger to be the bearer of the Constitution to Washington City. Dr. Menefee nominated Dr. J. H. Cocke; Mr. Ringgold nominated C. F. M. Noland; Dr. Drennen nominated R. C. S. Brown; Mr. Clarke of C. nominated Barnett Williams; Mr. Walker of H. nominated Elias Rector; Mr. Drew nominated Roberson Childress; and Mr. King nominated the US Mail. The convention then proceeded to the election, and on counting the ballots, there appeared on the several ballotings the following results.

	1	2	3	4	5	6	7
J. H. Cocke … … … … … … … …	4	6	6	5	--	--	--
C. F. M. Noland … … … … … …	9	10	10	13	16	25	28
R. C. S. Brown … … … … … …	13	15	15	10	19	20	20
B. Williams … … … … … … …	5	5	3	--	--	--	--
E. Rector … … … … … … … …	10	10	11	11	9	--	--
R. Childress … … … … … … …	4	3	3	4	5	4	1
US Mail … … … … … … … …	4	1	2	1	1	1	1

Mr. Williams was withdrawn on the fourth ballot, Dr. Cocke on the fifth, and Col. Childress on the seventh. And C. F. M. Noland, having received on the seventh ballot a majority of all the votes, was declared duly elected.

———————

Saturday, January 30, 1836

Mr. Whinnery moved that the Constitution, as read, be adopted, upon which the yeas and nays were called for and were as follows: yeas, 47; nays, 4. So the Constitution was adopted.

Work of the Constitutional Convention Completed

Mr. Bean submitted the following resolution, which was unanimously adopted: that the thanks of this convention are given to John Wilson for the able, dignified, and impartial manner in which he has discharged the duties devolving on him as president thereof.

Upon which, Mr. Wilson rose and addressed the convention, as follows.

Gentlemen, deeply impressed as I am with a high sense of gratitude, not only for your selection of me to preside over the deliberations of this highly respectable body but for the unanimous resolution that you have been pleased to adopt at the close of the solemn duties that the people have been pleased to confide to us, it is my sincere hope that the approbation of the community may crown the result of your labors and that it may accomplish the momentous object for which we have been convened and redound to the liberty, tranquility, and permanent welfare of our constituents and to prosperity. While I tender you my affectionate adieu (for indeed, gentlemen, it may be a final adieu with many of us), indulge me in fervent expression of my gratitude for your uniform support and approbation and my best wishes for your prosperity and happiness. My thanks are to you all, and my best wishes accompany you to your homes and domestic enjoyments.

Mr. Ball submitted the following resolution, which was unanimously adopted: that the president present the thanks of this convention to Charles P. Bertrand, secretary to the convention, for the able and faithful discharge of the duties of his office during the session of this convention.

Mr. Walker of Hempstead submitted the following resolution, which was adopted: that Messrs. Cummins, Fowler, and McLain, in connection with any other member of this convention who may remain in Little Rock, are requested to superintend the copying of the Constitution for Arkansas, and attaching the signatures thereto.

Mr. Farrelly introduced the following resolution which was adopted: that the president of this convention is instructed to address a note by the bearer of the Constitution to the secretary of state of the United States to accompany said Constitution, and that the secretary countersigns the same.

And on motion of Mr. Drennen, the convention then adjourned sine die.

The state map of Arkansas was "entered according to the Act of Congress" in the year of 1836, just one hundred years ago, by H. S. Tanner. The western boundary line does not correspond with the present boundary. The Fort Smith shown in what is now Oklahoma is the original fort and not the second fort and the city. What was then Miller County is now part of Texas. Some of the towns that appear on the map have passed away. Among them are Greenock, which was once Crittenden Court House in Crittenden County, and Lewisburg in Conway County, once a post for the stage lines and a port for the Arkansas River steamers. The mapmaker's Point Remove in Conway County, now identifiable only by the marker on the highway bridge crossing a small stream of the same name, was once known also as Peconery. It was near Morrilton, which is not shown on the 1836 map. Dardanelle is shown but in Pope County and on the wrong side of the Arkansas River. The Arkansas landings listed in the steamboat routes given in the margin of the map are: from Little Rock to New Orleans: Vaugine's Harrington's Arkansas (Post), Junction of Arkansas and Mississippi Rivers, Villemont; from Little Rock to Fort Gibson: Cadron, Lewisburg, "Petite Jean" River, Dwight, Dardanelle Mountain, Maycallin River, Caney Creek, Short Mt. Settlement, Pine Creek, Frog Creek, and Fort Smith.

Chapter 6

A Plea Made for Arkansas

June 9, 1836

Mr. Hamer[4] rose and addressed the chair as follows:

I will say a word in passing with regard to Arkansas. She is equally entitled to admission with the other (Michigan). Is her constitution republican? Who doubts it? Is this a time or place to discuss abstractions? If her constitution is not republican, then the constitutions of one half the states in the Union are not. Are we prepared to fan a flame that already burns with a strength and ardor calculated to startle every patriot in the land? I am sure that a large majority of this House will frown down all attempts to produce an excitement that can do no possible good and may be attended by evils of the most alarming character. You have given her a territorial government and engrafted institutions upon it by your own laws. She is on the southern side of the line drawn by the "compromise" of the Missouri question. She has asked you repeatedly for leave to form a state government, and you have neglected her, as you did Michigan. She has at length acted and framed a constitution that she respectfully asks you to accept and ratify and to allow her to come into the Union. How can she be refused? She has a requisite number of inhabitants. They are our friends and

---

4 Thomas L. Hamer, a representative from Ohio, was a native of Pennsylvania. He was admitted to the bar in 1821 and began the practice of law at Georgetown, Ohio. For several years he was a member of the lower house of the Ohio legislature, serving one term as speaker. He was elected as a Democrat to the Twenty-Third, Twenty-Fourth, and Twenty-Fifth Congresses, and he nominated Ulysses S. Grant as a cadet to West Point. He volunteered as a private in the war with Mexico and the next day was commissioned a brigadier general. He died in the service at Monterey, Mexico, on December 2, 1846, and on March 2, 1847, Congress adopted resolutions of sorrow and presented a sword to his nearest relative.

fellow citizens and entitled to a full participation in all the benefits of the Union.

With regard to objections to their constitution, the same remarks may be made that were applied to the other state. Compel them to change it. Admit them, and perhaps the next week they will call a convention and amend it, so as to restore the same features to which you raised the objection. The people of these new communities deserve kindness at our hands. They are under our protection and guardianship, and now, when they are about to set up for themselves, we ought to manifest the affection of a parent and the solicitude of a friend for their future welfare. By this means we shall secure their gratitude and esteem and rivet their attachment to a Union that, in its practical operation, dispenses so large an amount of individual and general happiness to the citizens of this great republic.

I shall vote, then, against the amendment now proposed, because it is unnecessary and its adoption may cause the bill to be lost in the Senate. I shall vote against all amendments that may be offered for the same reasons. As the bill now stands, it gives to Ohio all she asks and it provides amply for Michigan. There is not necessity for an alteration or amendment; and no one who is a friend to the principal features of the bill should risk its final defeat by voting to change its details. Let us adhere to it, as it came from the Senate. We have the whole subject now under our control. We can put an end to a most distracting contest that has agitated our country from Maine to Georgia and from the Atlantic to the most remote settlement upon the frontier. There was a time when the most painful anxiety pervaded the whole nation, and whilst each one waited with feverish impatience for further intelligence from the disputed territory, he trembled lest the ensuing mail should bear the disastrous tidings of a civil strife in which brother had fallen by the hand of brother and the soil of freedom had been stained by the blood of her own sons. But the storm has passed. The usual good fortune of the American people has prevailed. The land heaves in view, and a haven, with its widespread arms, invites us to enter. After so long an exposure to the fury of a tempest that was apparently gathering in our political horizon, let us seize the first opportunity to steer the ship into a safe harbor far beyond the reach of that elemental war that threatened her security in the open sea. Let us pass this bill. It does justice to all. It conciliates all. Its provisions will carry peace and harmony to those who are now agitated by strife and disquieted by tumults and disorders. By this just, humane, and beneficent policy, we shall consolidate our liberties and make this government what Mr. Jefferson, more than thirty years ago, declared it to be: "the strongest government on earth; the only one where every man, at the call of the law, will fly to the standard of the law, and meet invasions of the public order as his own personal concern." With this policy on the part of the government and the spirit of patriotism that now animates our citizens in full vigor, united America may bid defiance to a world in arms. Should Providence continue to smile upon our country, we may confidently anticipate that the freedom, happiness, and prosperity that we now enjoy will be as perpetual as the lofty mountains that crown our continent or the noble rivers that fertilize our plains.

Thursday, June 9, 1836

The bill for the admission of Michigan was then laid aside, and the bill for the admission of Arkansas was taken.

Mr. Phillips said it was now past midnight. Exhausted in body and mind, he did not feel that it was his duty to remain and consent to the precipitate action by which it was evidently intended to force through the committee the bills of the importance of those under consideration. He therefore moved the committee rise. The motion having been put, there were seventeen yeas and ninety-two nays—not a quorum.

Mr. Sevier requested Mr. Phillips to withdraw his motion.

Mr. Phillips said that if, with a knowledge of the fact that a quorum was not present, he could be persuaded to withdraw his motion, or to refrain from insisting that the chairman rise and report the fact to the House, according to its rules, for the purpose of acting upon a bill to admit a state into the Union, he should feel himself unworthy of the place he held. The committee than rose and reported the fact that they were without a quorum.

Mr. Reed moved an adjournment on which, on the motion of Mr. Sevier, the yeas and nays were ordered.

Mr. Adams requested that the hour (near one o'clock) might be noted on the journal.

The speaker said it was not in order.

The question on the adjournment being taken, the vote was twenty-four yeas and ninety-eight nays. There being a quorum, the House again went into committee upon the bill for the admission of Arkansas.

Mr. L. Williams moved to amend the bill, so as to reduce the judge's salary for that district to $1,500. A motion was again made that the committee rise, and the vote was fifteen yeas and ninety-five nays—again not a quorum. The members having been counted, 112 were reported present.

Mr. Sevier said he did not wish to press the bill at the late hour of the night. When the committee had risen, he said he should be satisfied if the House would make the bill the special order for tomorrow at ten o'clock. There were loud cries of "No, no!" The committee rose and reported that they were without a quorum. A motion was made to adjourn, which was lost.

A call of the House was ordered at near half past one o'clock. At about half past four, 112 members having answered and several absentees having been sent for and brought up in custody of the sergeant at arms, a motion to excuse all the absentees prevailed, and the doors were opened. The House again went into Committee of the Whole and resumed the consideration of the Arkansas bill.

Mr. Adams moved to amend the bill by introducing a clause that "nothing in this act shall be construed as an assent by Congress to the article in the constitution of the said state in relation to slavery and the emancipation of slaves." This motion was debated at some extent by Mr. Adams.

Mr. Cushing then addressed the committee. Mr. Hard[5] rose to oppose the bill and advocate the amendment but said, as the committee had been in session twenty hours and every member must feel seriously the fatigue of this long session, and as the bill had been taken up for consideration since twelve o'clock at night, he hoped the committee would rise to enable those who wished to give their views of the measure an opportunity to examine more carefully the bill and other papers and documents connected with it. The committee refused to rise by a large majority.

Mr. Briggs said that after having sat there twelve hours, he left the House, exhausted, at ten o'clock last evening. At daylight that morning he was notified by one of the messengers of the House that his attendance was again desired. When he entered the hall, he learned that the committee had just taken up the bill for the admission of Arkansas into the Union. His respected colleague across the way (Mr. Adams) was upon the floor, having just offered amendment to the bill. That amendment related to an article in the constitution of Arkansas on the subject of slavery. He knew the committee had dragged out a long,

---

5   Gideon Hard of Albion, New York, was representative of the Forty-Second New York District in the Twenty-Third and Twenty-Fourth Congresses. He served also as a member of the New York State Senate from 1842 to 1847 and as county judge of Orleans County from 1856 to 1860.

weary night and were worn down with their protracted labors. Yet, such was the magnitude of the subject, he felt himself impelled by an imperious sense of duty to submit a few remarks for the consideration of the committee.

It must be seen at a glance that this simple, plain declaration (Mr. Adam's amendment) contains nothing of the principle which gave rise to the Missouri controversy. In that case a restriction was imposed upon Missouri which denied to that state certain rights and powers that, under the constitution of the United States, were possessed by other states. The advocates of the state contended that Congress had no authority to enforce that restriction, or limitation, upon her sovereignty. This amendment does not, in the slightest degree, abridge, restrain, or in any manner interfere with the prerogative or power of Arkansas as an independent state. If adopted, it will not postpone her admission into the Union a single day. It does not question the right of her citizens to any species of property recognized by the constitution or laws of the state. It imposes no restraint upon her political power and sovereignty. It simply denies that, by the act of admitting her into the Union with this article incorporated into her constitution, Congress gives its assent to the principles of that article. Without this protestation, the act of admission would be at least an implied assent to this extraordinary constitutional provision. Whilst such an approbation would be of no use or benefit to that state, it would be in direct violation of the opinion of a large majority of the members of the House and the known sentiments of the people which they represent. The debate was further continued by Mr. Wise.

The question was then taken at about four o'clock in the morning, and the amendment was negative by a vote of ninety-eight to thirty-two. Mr. Adams moved that the committee rise. He lost by forty-four to ninety-three.

Mr. Harlan[6] moved an amendment: "Amend in section five, line three, by striking out 2,000 and inserting 1,500. In the fourth line, add, after the word 'his,' the words 'acceptance of the,' so as to make the section read as follows: 'Sec. 5. And be it further enacted that there shall be allowed to the judge of the said district court the annual compensation of $1,500, to commence from the date of his acceptance of the appointment, to be paid quarter-yearly at the Treasury of the United States.'"

Mr. Harlan remarked that, in submitting this amendment for consideration, it was not his intention to detain the committee at this early hour in the morning. He asked the indulgence of the committee, however, to make a very brief explanation of his object in offering the amendment.

The bill provides for the appointment of a district judge at an annual salary of $2,000 commence from the date of his appointment. The amendment proposed by him reduces the salary to $1,500 per annum, to commence from the date of the acceptance of the office.

There are now three judges in Arkansas, who perform all the business of the territory at a salary of $1,200 each. When it becomes a state, nearly the whole of the business will be performed by the state courts. The present judges have very extensive circuits and necessarily spend much of their time and money in traveling to different parts of the territory. No complaint has been heard from them of the inadequacy of their compensation.

---

6 James Harlan was born in Mercer County in Kentucky on June 22, 1800, and began practicing law in Harrisburg in 1823. He was prosecuting attorney in 1829 and representative of the Fifth Kentucky District in the Twenty-Fourth and Twenty-Fifth Congresses. He was secretary of state of Kentucky from 1840 to 1844 and was appointed attorney general of the state in 1850. He held this office until his death at Frankfort on February 18, 1863.

The compensation proposed by the bill to be given to the district judge exceeds that given to the same officer in many of the states of this Union. The district judge in each of the states of Connecticut, Rhode Island, New Jersey, Delaware, Tennessee, and Kentucky received an annual compensation of $1,500; in Vermont and Missouri, $1,200; and in New Hampshire, Ohio, Indiana, and Illinois, $1,000. It is not pretended that the duties to be performed by the district judge of Arkansas will be more laborious or difficult than in either of the states above mentioned. Why, then, the disproportion in the compensation?

"It seems to me," said Mr. Harlan, "that there is a concerted movement by many of the officers of this government to procure an increase of their salaries. The army of clerks in this city has moved in solid column to affect that object. The honorable gentleman from Tennessee (Mr. C. Johnson), who has heretofore been so generally uniform in his opposition to an increase of salaries and extravagant expenditure of the public money, has reported a bill from the Committee of Ways and Means, reducing the number of clerks from 366 to 321 and giving to the latter about $80,000 annually, more than were paid to the former number. If this be one of the modes of distributing the surplus money in the treasury, it will not obtain my assent. The offices of the federal government at the present salaries are sought after with much avidity; but whenever it is ascertained that the services of persons competent to discharge the duties cannot be obtained at the present salaries, then, and not till then, will be the proper time to increase them.

"I object to that part of this bill that provides that the salary of the judge to be appointed shall commence from the date of the appointment. If the amendment which I have had the honor to purpose prevails, the salary will commence from the time of the acceptance of the office, instead of from the date of the commission. The presumption is that a citizen of Arkansas will receive the appointment. Several months will necessarily elapse from the time of signing the commission by the president and the acceptance by the appointee. During that time the judge is to be paid—and for what? He now only will not have rendered any services, but he will be wholly ignorant of his appointment. If one who is not in the pay of the government should be appointed, he will receive his salary to the date of his resignation and be entitled by this bill to receive the salary of the new office from the date of the commission. It seems to me that the compensation of an officer ought to commence from the time he intimates his readiness to engage in the public service, by accepting an appointment, and not from the time the president decides on the appointment."

The amendment was rejected; there were thirty-two yeas and no nays counted. The Arkansas bill was then laid aside, and the committee took up the "supplementary bill for the admission of Arkansas into the Union and for other purposes."

Mr. Mason of Virginia moved that the committee rise and report the two Michigan and Arkansas bills to the House. Considerable confusion arose as to whether the Michigan bill had been ordered to be reported to the House or merely laid aside and was still open to amendment.

Mr. Mason withdrew his motion, and Mr. Underwood moved an amendment prescribing certain other conditions on which Michigan should be admitted. He lost.

Mr. Mason of Virginia renewed the motion that the committee rise and report the bills to the House. (This was about seven o'clock.)

Mr. Slade[7] moved to amend the Arkansas bill: "After the words in the first section, 'that the state of Arkansas shall be one and is hereby declared to be one of the United States of America and admitted into the Union on an equal footing with the original states in all respects,' add, 'whenever the people of said state shall be a convention, duly elected, expunge from its present constitution so much thereof as prohibits the general assembly from passing laws for emancipation of slaves without the consent of the owners; and shall also provide in and by said constitution that no Negro or mulatto, born in or brought into said state after its admission into the Union, shall be held or transferred as property or in any way subjected to slavery or involuntary servitude, unless in punishment for crimes committed against the laws of said state, whereof the party accused shall be duly convicted.'"

Mr. Cave Johnson made a question to order. The Arkansas bill, having been laid aside, was not open to amendment.

Mr. E. Whittlesey[8] appealed to the gentleman from Vermont to withdraw the amendment, one of the same tenor having been offered by the gentleman from Massachusetts (Mr. Adams) and rejected.

---

7   William Slade was born in Cornwall, Vermont, on May 9, 1786. After graduating from Middlebury College in 1808, he studied law, was admitted to the bar, and began practicing in Middlebury in 1810. He established the *Columbian Patriot* and edited it from 1814 to 1816, and he served five years as secretary of state of Vermont. He was elected as a Whig to the Twenty-Second and the five succeeding Congresses. He was governor of Vermont from 1845 to 1846 and died in Middlebury on January 18, 1859.

8   Elisha Whittlesey, a representative from Ohio, was born in Washington, Connecticut, on October 19, 1783. In 1806, he moved to Ohio and began the practice of law in Canfield. He was prosecuting attorney for his county for sixteen years, served in the War of 1812, and served in the state House of Representatives from 1820 to 1821. He was elected to the Eighteenth and seven succeeding Congresses, resigning on July 9, 1838. He was auditor for the Post Office Department from 1841 to 1849. He was appointed comptroller of the treasury by President Taylor and served from 1849 to 1857. He was removed by President Buchanan but reappointed by President Lincoln in 1861 and served until his death in Washington on January 7, 1863.

Mr. Slade declined and addressed the House in support of the motion. Mr. Jennifer rose to reply and proceeded to make some general remarks on the subject of the abolition movements, when he was called to order by Mr. Bynum and others, on the grounds that his remarks were irrelevant. After some words between Messrs. Jennifer and Bynum, the motion of Mr. Slade was rejected.

Mr. Wish then rose and addressed the House at length in opposition to the course of the majority, in pressing this question upon a House that was sleepy, tired, and drunk. He was opposed to the motion that the committee report the bills and said he would speak till ten o'clock, when the House would be under the necessity of dropping the subject, as it was not a special order for Friday. Mr. Wise several times gave way to motions that the committee rise, which were lost without a count. At half past nine, Mr. Wise yielded the floor.

Mr. McKennan[9] suggested that, as the members were much exhausted, the committee should rise with the understanding that the House should then adjourn till tomorrow, when the gentleman from Virginia would resume his remarks.

Mr. Wise said that it was true that he was in an unfit condition to continue his remarks, but it was near ten o'clock and he had it in his power to have his will over this subject. So help him God, he would persevere. He proceeded in his remarks till ten o'clock.

---

9 Thomas McKean Thompson McKennan, a representative from Pennsylvania, was born in Newcastle County in Delaware on March 31, 1794. He was a graduate of Washington and Jefferson, class of 1810, and was admitted to the bar four years later, beginning his legal career in Washington, Pennsylvania. From 1815 to 1816 he was deputy attorney general of the state and was elected as a Whig of the Twenty-Second, Twenty-Third, Twenty-Fourth, Twenty-Fifth, and Twenty-Seventh Congresses. He was appointed secretary of the interior by President Filmore, serving from August 15 to September 12 in 1850. He died in Reading, Pennsylvania, on July 9, 1852.

Mr. Chambers of Kentucky then rose, Mr. Wise having temporarily yielded the floor, and called upon the chair to decide whether the committee could continue to sit. Mr. Wise asked where the Speaker of the House was. "In his room," was answered by someone.

Mr. Denny called for the reading of the rules of the House, respecting the daily adjournment and meeting of the House. Mr. Whittlesey suggested to the chair whether, in the case of bills made the order of the day for a particular portion of the day, it had not been the uniform practice, when the limited time expired, for the chairman of the committee to leave the chair to allow the House to proceed on its other business.

Mr. Wise called for the reading of the resolution by which the bills now before the committee were made the special order of the day. The resolution was read, "making the bill to establish the northern boundary of Ohio and the bills for the admission of Michigan and Arkansas into the Union, the special order of the day for Wednesday next, and each day thereafter, Fridays and Saturdays accepted, until the same be disposed of."

Mr. McKennan called for the reading of a resolution, passed some weeks ago (and it was read), providing that, after a certain day, the daily sittings of the House shall commence at ten o'clock in the morning.

Mr. Whittlesey called for the reading of one of the standing rules of the House, and it was read: "Touching the duties of the speaker—he shall take the chair every day precisely at the hour to which the House shall have adjourned on the preceding day; shall immediately call the members to order; and, on the appearance of a quorum, shall cause the journal of the preceding day to be read."

Mr. Love said he would, with permission of the chair, ask the question whether, if the committee refused to rise and sat on until tomorrow, the members of the House would be considered as entitled to pay for two days' or for one day's service.

Mr. McKennan asked of the chair, as a question of order, whether it was not the duty of the speaker to take the chair every day on the arrival of the hour of ten o'clock. The chairman said that he should not undertake in his present place (of chairman of the Committee of the Whole) to decide any question in reference to the duty of the Speaker of the House.

Mr. McKennan then moved that the committee rise for the purpose of deciding in the House that question.

Mr. Pickens called for the reading of the 105 and 106 rules of the House; and they were read: "the House shall be observed in a Committee of the Whole House, so far as they may be applicable, except the rule limiting the time of speaking; but no member shall speak twice on any question until every member choosing to speak shall have spoken.

"No standing rule or order of the House shall be rescinded or changed without one day's notice being given of the motion therefore. Nor shall any rule be suspended, except by a vote of at least two-thirds of the members present. Nor shall the order of business, as established by the rules of the House, be postponed or changed, except by a vote of at least two-thirds of the members present."

Mr. Bell said he did not know, nor was it material to what he rose to say, what object could be accomplished by prolonging the present sitting; but it was, in his opinion, the duty of the committee to rise in order to decide the question of order now raised. A majority of the committee might indeed oblige the committee to continue in session, but they would do it in defiance of the express rule of the House. There was no alternative in the present case, under the rules, but for the committee to rise. It would be in the power of the majority, when in the House, to direct the continuation of the discussion to which, for his part (Mr. Bell said), he should not object. But he begged of gentlemen to respect not the parliamentary law but the positive written rules of the House.

Mr. Glascock[10] said there had, in the present case, been no adjournment from yesterday's sitting, and that the practice of courts of justice, in similar cases, would be a proper rule for this House. The day's sitting should be considered to extend to the time of adjournment. The principle contended for by gentlemen could not apply in the present case because there had been no adjournment.

Mr. Mason of Virginia suggested, as a mode of freeing the House from its present embarrassment, that the committee should now rise and let these bills be made the special order for the day, so that they would come up again as a matter of course on the House resuming its sitting after an adjournment. The question was taken on the motion which had been made for the committee to rise and determined in the negative.

Mr. Wise then resumed the thread of his remarks upon the bill, and having concluded,

Mr. McKennan obtained the floor. The members of the House were, he said, evidently all worn out by this protracted sitting; many had not slept, and others had not broken their fast. All had need of repose. "We have," said he, "fought the bill manfully, and done our best to stave off the decision upon it. My friend from Virginia (especially) has fought it hard and long and has, in fact, verified the old adage 'a

---

10 Thomas Glascock, a representative from Georgia, was a lieutenant with the American forces in the Revolutionary War, and he also served in the campaign against the Creek Indians. He was elected to the Twenty-Fourth and Twenty-Fifth Congresses and died in Decatur, Georgia, on May 9, 1841.

lean dog for a long chase.' I hope, sir, the committee will rise and report the bills, and that we shall adjourn over till tomorrow."

Mr. McKennan made a motion to this effect. The motion was carried. The committee rose and reported the two bills, and the House then adjourned over to meet on Saturday at the usual hour.

Chapter 7

Arkansas Bill Passed

Monday, June 13, 1836, Michigan and Arkansas

In execution of the special order of Monday last, the House then proceeded to the consideration of the following bills: "An act to establish the northern boundary of the state of Ohio and to provide for the admission of the state of Michigan into the Union upon the conditions therein expressed.

"An act for the admission of the state of Arkansas into the Union, and to provide for the due execution of the laws of the United States within the same and for other purposes."

Both these bills had been reported from the Committee of the Whole without amendment.

Arkansas

The House then took up the bill providing for the admission of Arkansas into the Union.

Mr. Briggs asked for the yeas and nays, which were ordered. Mr. Adams then renewed the amendment submitted by him in the Committee of the Whole in relation to the restriction of slavery in the state of Arkansas. The amendment having been read, Mr. Williams of Kentucky[11] rose and moved the previous question. Mr. Adams then claimed the floor.

---

11 Sherrod Williams was a native of Kentucky and received his education in that state. He was elected to represent the Fourth Kentucky District as a member of the Twenty-Fourth Congress, convening March 4, 1835, and was reelected to the Twenty-Fifth and Twenty-Sixth Congresses, serving until March 3, 1841.

After a discussion on procedure, the House adopted a motion for the previous question. The bill was ordered to a third reading by a vote of 147 to 52. The Michigan bill was then read a third time. Mr. Vanderpoel said that a test vote had already been taken upon this bill, and the expression in its favor was so strong that no gentleman could doubt its passage. Under a firm belief that the further consumption of time would not change a vote, or alter the result, he moved the previous question. So the bill was passed.

The Arkansas bill was then taken up and read a third time. Mr. Huntsman moved the previous question, which was seconded with ninety-five yeas and no nays, and the main question being ordered. Mr. Allen of Vermont then asked for the yeas and nays on the passage of the bill, which were ordered—yeas, 143; nays, 50—and as follows:

Yeas: Messrs. Chilton, Allan, Ash, Ashley, Barton, Beale, Bean, Bockee, Boon, Bouldin, Body, Brown, Buchanan, Bunche, Burns, John Calhoon, Cambreleng, Campbell, Carter, Casey, George Chambers, John Chambers, Chane, Chapman, Chapin, Nathaniel H. Claiborne, John F. H. Claiborne, Cleveland, Coffee, Coles, Connor, Craig, Cramer, Cushman, Deberry, Dickson, Doubleday, Dromgoole, Fairfield, Farlin, French, Fry, William K. Fuller, Galbraith, James Garland, Rice Garland, Fillet, Grantland, Graves, Grayson, Griffin, Haley, J. Hall, Hamer, Hardin, Harlan, Albert G. Harrison, Hawes, Hawkins, Haynes, Holsey, Hopkins, Howard, Howell, Hubley, Huntington, Huntsman, Ingham, Jabez Jackson, Jarvis, Joseph Johnson, Richard M. Johnson, Cave Johnson, Henry Johnson, John W. Jones, Judson, Kilgore, Kinnard, Lane, Lansing, Lawler, Gideon Lee, Joshua Lee, Luke Lea, Leonard, Lewis, Logan, Loyall, Lucas, Lyon, Abijah Job Mann, Martin, John Y. Mason, William Mason, Moses Mason, Maurcy, McComas, McKay, McKeon, McKim, McLene, Miller, Montgomery, Morgan, Muhlenberg, Owens, Page, Parks, Patterson, Patton, Franklin Pierce, Phelps, Pinckney, Rencher, John Reynolds, Joseph Reynolds, Ripley, Roane, Robertson, Rogers, Seymour, Augustine H. Shepperd,

Shields, Sickles, Smith, Spangler, Speight, Standefer, Storer, Taliaferro, Taylor, Thomas, Toucey, Turrill, Vanderpoel, Ward, Washington, Webster, Weeks, White, Thomas T. Whittlesey, Sherrod, Williams, and Wise

Nays: Messrs. Adams, Hemen, Allen, Anthony, Bailey, Bond, Borden, Briggs, William B. Calhound, Childs, Clark, Crane, Cushing, Darlington, Denny, Evans, Everett, Phil C. Fuller, Grennell, Hall, Hard, Harper, Hazletine, Henderson, Hiester, Hoar, William Jackson, James, Benjamin Jones, Laporte, Lawrence, Lay, Lincoln, Love, Samson Mason, McCarty, McKennan, Morris, Parker, Dutee J. Pearce, Phillips, Potts, Reed, Russell, Shinn, Slade, John Thomson, Underwood, Vinton, Elisha Whittlesey, and Lewis Williams

So the bill was passed. Mr. Connor said, as the House had been delivered of twins, he thought after the operation they might adjourn. He made that motion but subsequently withdrew it as the request of Mr. Claiborne of Mississippi, who made an ineffectual attempt to offer a resolution. Mr. Love renewed the motion to adjourn, and the House adjourned.

West Boundary of the State

Tuesday, June 14, 1836, Michigan and Arkansas

On the motion of Mr. Sevier, the House went into the Committee of the Whole on the state of the Union (Mr. Pierce of New Hampshire in the chair) and proceeded to consider the following bill: "An act supplementary to the act for the admission of the state of Arkansas into the Union, and to provide for the due execution of the laws of the United States within the same, and for other purposes."

The bill having been read, Mr. Vinton[12] moved the following amendment, as an additional section to the bill: Be it further enacted, that the eighth section of an ordinance passed by the convention of delegates at Little Rock, assembled for the purpose of making a constitution for the state of Arkansas, which is in the following words: "All that section of the country lying west of the western boundary of the state of Arkansas, which was formerly a part of the Territory of Arkansas under the provisions of an act of Congress, approved the twenty-sixty day of May, 1824, entitled 'An act to fix the western boundary line of the Territory of Arkansas,' and which was ceded by the United States to the Cherokee and Choctaw Indians, whenever the Indian title shall be extinguished to the same, shall be attached to and form a part of the state of Arkansas; and when the said Indian title shall be extinguished, the western boundary of the said state shall be in accordance with the provisions of the said act of Congress."

Mr. Vinton addressed the committee at some length in support of the amendment.

A debate followed in which Messrs. Sevier, Parker, Love, Patton, Chambreleng, Howard, Huntsman, Standefer, McKay, Toucey, and Chambers of Pennsylvania took part. (Mr. Cushing, who spoke at length, said he would have this proposition of the convention of Arkansas "stamped at once with the probation of Congress.")

Mr. Vinton withdrew his amendment, and offered the following: Strike out the word "that" in the first section of the bill and insert, "In

---

12 Samuel Finley Vinton was born in South Hadley, Massachusetts, on September 25, 1792. He graduated from Williams College in 1816, studied law, and was admitted to the bar two years later. He then moved to Ohio and began practicing in Gallipolis. He held several local offices and was elected to the Eighteenth and the six succeeding Congresses. Later he was reelected to the Twenty-Eighth and the three succeeding Congresses. In 1862 he was appointed by President Lincoln to appraise the slaves emancipated in the District of Columbia. He died in Washington on May 11, 1862.

lieu of the proposition submitted to Congress by the ordinance of the convention of delegates, held at Little Rock, assembled for the purpose of making a constitution, which is hereby rejected." After a few remarks from Messrs. Toucey, Chambers of Pennsylvania, and Sevier, it was agreed to.

The bill was then laid aside, and the committee took up the "bill supplementary to the act to establish the northern boundary line of Ohio, and to provide for the admission of Michigan into the Union." The bill having been read, Mr. Vinton moved the same amendment to this bill he had moved to the Arkansas bill, and which had been agreed to, merely changing the words "Arkansas" and "Little Rock" to "Michigan" and "Detroit."

After some remarks from Messrs. Garland of Louisiana, Sevier, Roberston, Vinton, Lane, and Huntsman, the amendment was agreed to. The speaker having resumed the chair, the House concurred in the amendment of the Committee of the Whole to the Arkansas bill, and the same was ordered to be engrossed for a third reading tomorrow.

––––––––

June 15, 1836, Michigan and Arkansas

The following engrossed bills were then read a third time and passed: the bill supplementary to the act entitled "An act to establish the northern boundary line of Ohio and to provide the admission of the state of Michigan into the Union"; an act supplementary to the act entitled "An act for the admission of the state of Arkansas into the Union, and to provide for the due execution of the laws of the United States with the same, and for other purposes"; and the bill to provide for the due execution of the laws of the United States within the state of Michigan.

Steps in the Fixing of Arkansas's West Boundary

The statutory western boundary of Arkansas in 1819, the boundary fixed by law, was the western line of the Louisiana Purchase. At that time Arkansas Territory included almost all the present states of Arkansas and Oklahoma. The civil boundary, the line marking the western limit of the jurisdiction of the territorial government, was east of the statutory boundary.

On December 17, 1823, Senator Thomas H. Benton of Missouri presented in the Senate a memorial of the Arkansas Territory General Assembly, protesting against the proposed fixing of the boundary as a line due south from the southwest corner of the state of Missouri to the Red River. On March 23, 1824, Senator Benton reported a bill to fix the boundary forty miles west of the one suggested in the act of 1823. Senator Benton's bill passed the Senate, but in the House there was strong opposition. Henry W. Conway, Arkansas's delegate, took charge of the measure. The bill as passed on May 26 established as the western boundary a line beginning at a point forty miles west of the southwest corner of the state of Missouri and running south to the right bank of the Red River and thence down that river with the (then) Mexican boundary to the line of the state of Louisiana.

The Choctaw Indians protested, and a treaty concluded on January 20, 1825, ceded to the United States their lands east of a line beginning on the Arkansas, one hundred paces east of old Fort Smith (not the present city), running thence due south to the Red River and then northeast to Point Remove on the Arkansas River. The treaty of 1828, with the Cherokees north of the Arkansas River, ceded to the United States all their claims in Arkansas as now bounded. By treaty the Choctaws were reassured concerning the boundary agreed upon in 1825. The western boundary of Arkansas was fixed as a line commencing on the Red River at a point where the eastern Choctaw line strikes that river and runs due north with that line to the Arkansas River, and thence directly to the southwest corner of Missouri. This treaty, together with that concluded with the Choctaw in 1825, cut off a strip forty miles wide along the entire western border of Arkansas Territory for the boundary fixed by Congress in 1824. It severed from Arkansas a large part of Lovely County in the northwest, as the Choctaw treaty cut off much of Crawford and Miller Counties south of the Arkansas.

A resurvey of the entire western line in 1877 showed the Choctaw line as run in 1825 diverged to the west for a due south course and thus threw into Arkansas 137,500 acres that belonged to the Indians, and that the Cherokee survey of 1831–32 north of the river diverged to the west and put 2,539 acres of the Indians' land in Arkansas. The Indians were compensated for these losses.

Text of Bill Admitting Arkansas

The following is the bill as it passed the Senate:

A bill for the admission of the state of Arkansas into the Union, and to provide for the due execution of the laws of the United States within the same, and for other purposes. Whereas the people of the Territory of Arkansas did, on the thirtieth day of January, in the present year by a convention of delegates called and assembled for that purpose, form for themselves a constitution and state government, which constitution and state government, so formed, is republican; and whereas the number of inhabitants within the said territory exceeds forty-seven thousand seven hundred persons, computed according to the rule prescribed by the Constitution of the United States; and the said convention have, in their behalf, asked the Congress of the United States to admit the said territory into the Union as a state, on an equal footing with the original States.

Be it enacted, that the state of Arkansas shall be one, and is hereby declared to be one of the United States of America and admitted into the Union on an equal footing with the original States, in all respects whatever; and the said state shall consist of all the territory included within the following boundaries, to wit: beginning in the middle of the main channel of the Mississippi River, on the parallel of thirty-six degrees north latitude; running from thence west, with the said parallel of latitude to the St. Francis River; thence, up the middle of the main channel of said river, to the parallel of thirty-six degrees thirty minutes north; from thence, west to the southwest corner of the state of Missouri; and from thence, to be bounded on the west, to the north bank of Red River, by "the lines described in the first article of the treaty made between the United States and the Cherokee nation of Indians west of the Mississippi, on the twenty-sixth of May, in the year of our Lord one thousand eight hundred and twenty-eight"; and to be bounded on the south side of Red River by the Mexican boundary line, to the northwest corner, of the state of Louisiana; thence, east, with the Louisiana State line, to the middle of the main channel of the Mississippi River; thence, up the middle of the main channel of the said river, to the thirty-sixth degree of north latitude, the point of beginning.

Section 2. *And be it further enacted* that until the next general census shall be taken, the said state shall be entitled to one representative in the House of Representatives of the United States.

Section 3. *And be it further enacted* that all the laws of the United States which are not locally inapplicable shall have the same force and effect within the said state of Arkansas as elsewhere within the United States.

Section 4. *And be it further enacted* that the said state shall be one judicial district and be called the Arkansas district; and a district court shall be held therein to consist of one judge, who shall reside in the said district and be called a district judge. He shall hold, at the seal of government of the said state, two sessions annually, on the first Mondays of April and November; and he shall in all things, have and exercise the same jurisdiction and powers which were, by law, given to the judge of the Kentucky district, under an act entitled "An act to establish the judicial courts of the United States." We shall appoint a clerk for the said district court, who shall reside and keep the records of the court at the place of holding the same; and shall receive, for the services performed by him, the same fees to which the clerk of the Kentucky district is entitled for similar services.

Section 5. *And be it further enacted* that there shall be allowed to the judge of the said district court the annual compensation of $2,000, to commence from the date of his appointment, to be paid quarter-yearly, at the Treasury of the United States.

Section 6. *And be it further enacted* that there shall be appointed in said district a person learned in the law to act as attorney for the United States, who shall, in addition to his stated fees, be paid by the United States $200, as a full compensation for all extra services.

Section 7. *And be it further enacted* that a marshal shall be appointed for the said district, who shall perform the same duties, be subject to the same regulations and penalties, and be entitled to the same fees as are prescribed to marshals in other districts; and he shall, moreover, be entitled to the sum of $200 annually, as a compensation for all extra services.

Section 8. *And be it further enacted* that the state of Arkansas is admitted into the Union upon the express condition that the people of the said state shall never interfere with the primary disposal of the public lands within the said state, nor shall they levy a tax on any of the lands of the United States within the said state; and nothing in this act shall be construed as an assent by Congress to all or to any of the propositions contained in the ordinance of the said convention of the people of Arkansas, nor to deprive the said state of Arkansas of the same grants, subject to the same restrictions, which were made to the state of Missouri by virtue of an act entitled "An act to authorize the people of the Missouri Territory to form a constitution and state government, and for the admission of such state into the Union on an equal footing with the original states, and to prohibit slavery in certain territories," approved the sixth day of March, one thousand eight hundred and twenty.

Michigan's Admission to the Union

Although a constitution for what is now the state of Michigan was framed at a convention in Detroit in May 1835 and adopted by popular vote in October, when state officers were elected and application for admission made. Michigan did not become a state until January 26, 1837. The delay was occasioned by a boundary dispute with Ohio. The ordinance creating the Northwest Territory had fixed the boundary line as claimed by Michigan, but when the constitution of Ohio was adopted, it was accompanied by a proviso designed to secure a northern boundary north of the Maumee River. After a "bloodless war" between the two for the possession of Toledo, Congress decided in Ohio's favor and gave Michigan the area now known as the Upper Peninsula. The boundary as fixed by Congress was rejected by a convention which met in Ann Arbor on September 4, a convention of the Jackson party, but was approved by a convention meeting in Ann Arbor on December 6. Congress held the action of the latter convention to be authoritative and admitted Michigan to statehood on January 26, 1837.

Ambrose H. Sevier and Statehood

In "The Constitution of 1836," Jesse Turner wrote the following:

The mind of Sevier was capacious and practical. He was neither a laggard nor a rash anticipator. Animated by a not ignoble opportunism, he had, in the contest on which were staked the destinies of the young state, played his part with consummate address—always alert, discerning, and resourceful. He had at this conjuncture, it is true, powerful and loyal allies: Woodruff and Pike and Ashley (*clarum et venerabile nomen!*), and Fowler, and Walker and Scott, and Bates, and scores of other able, patriotic and farseeing men, all encouraged and supported by an overwhelming public sentiment. Nevertheless, on a general survey of the field, and after all legitimate deductions have been made, Sevier still stands the protagonist of the statehood era. Nay, more, his just fame rises yet higher. So conspicuous and sustained was the ability which in his high place he continued to display until, with his sum still in its meridian splendor, his earthly career closed, that, to this day, and in the long perspective of more than seventy years, he looms one of the very few dominant figures in the annals of the commonwealth.[13]

Caleb Cushing's Address

A Massachusetts member protested against acceptance of the clause in the Arkansas Constitution, restricting the power of the legislature over slavery, and approved the amendment offered by John Quincy Adams.

In addressing the Committee of the Whole on the night of June 9, 1836, when the bill for the admissions of Arkansas was under consideration, Mr. Cushing of Massachusetts[14] said in part:

---

13 Jesse Turner, "The Constitution of 1836, *Publications of the Arkansas Historical Association, Volume 3.*

14 Cushing, born in Salisbury, Massachusetts, on January 17, 1800, graduated from Harvard at the age of seventeen. After his admission to the bar and ten years' service in the Massachusetts legislature as representative and senator, he was elected to the Twenty-Fourth Congress and reelected in the three following sessions. In 1843 he was appointed by President Tyler as commissioner to China, serving two years. He was colonel of a Massachusetts regiment in the war with Mexico and was appointed a brigadier general by President Polk. President Pierce appointed him attorney general of the United States in 1853, and in 1860 he was appointed by President Grant as counsel for the United States before the Geneva tribunal of arbitration on the Alabama claims. He was minister to Spain from1874 to 1877 and died in Newburyport, Massachusetts, on January 2, 1879.

Mr. Chairman, the House has now continued in session for the space of eighteen or nineteen hours without any interval of refreshment or rest. It is impossible to mistake the intentions of the ruling majority. I see clearly that the committee is resolved to sit out the debate on these important bills for the admission of Michigan and Arkansas into the Union. This, it is apparent, the majority have the power as well as the right to do. Whether it be just and reasonable is another question. I shall not quarrel, however, with the avowed will of the House. It has done me the favor to hear me with patience on other occasions; and I cannot render it the unfit return of trespassing on its indulgence at this unseasonable hour, nor seek to defeat its purposes by speaking against time. But having been charged with sundry memorials from citizens of Massachusetts and New Hampshire, remonstrating against that clause in the constitution of Arkansas which relates to the subject of slavery, I should be recreant to the trust they have reposed in me if I suffered the bill for the admission of Arkansas to pass without a word of protestation. The extraordinary circumstances under which I rise to address the committee impel me to brevity and succinctness, but they would afford me no justification for a passive acquiescence in the admission of Arkansas into the Union, with all the sins of its constitution upon its head.

The constitution of Arkansas, as communicated to Congress in the memorial of the people of that territory praying to be admitted into the Union, contains the following clause: "The General Assembly shall have no power to pass laws for the emancipation of slaves without the consent of the owners. They shall have no power to prevent emigrants to this state from bringing with them such persons as are deemed slaves by the laws of anyone of the United States."

The provision of the constitution of Arkansas is condemned by those whom I represent on this occasion as antirepublican, as wrong on general principles of civil polity, and as unjust to the inhabitants of the nonslaveholding states. They object to it as being, in effect, a provision to render slavery perpetual in the new state of Arkansas.

I concur in reprobating such a clause. The legislature of Arkansas is forbidden to emancipate the slaves within its jurisdiction, even though it should be ready to indemnify their owners. It is forbidden to exclude slaves from being imported into the state. I cannot, by any vote of mine, ratify or sanction a constitution of government which undertakes in this way to foreclose in advance the progress of civilization and of liberty forever.

In order to do justice to the unchangeable opinions of the North, without, in any respect, invading the rights, real or supposed, of the South, my colleague (Mr. Adams), the vigilant eye of whose unsleeping mind there is nothing which escapes, has moved an amendment of the bill for the admission of Arkansas into the Union, so that, if the amendment be adopted, the bill would read as follows: "The state of Arkansas is admitted into the Union upon the express condition that the people of the said state shall never interfere with the primary disposal of the public lands within the said state, nor shall they levy a tax on any of the lands of the United States within the said state; and nothing in this act shall be construed as an assent by Congress (to the article in the constitution of the said state relating to slavery and to the emancipation of the slaves), or to all or to any of the propositions contained in the ordinance of the said convention of the people of Arkansas, nor to deprive the state of Arkansas of the same grants, subject to the same restrictions, which were made to the state of Missouri."

This amendment is, according to my judgment, reasonable and proper in itself, and the very least that any member from the North can propose in vindication of the opinions and principles of himself and his constituents.

The gentleman from Virginia, who, I cheerfully admit, is always frank and honorable in his course upon this floor, has just declared that, as a Southern man, he had felt it to be his duty to come forward and take a stand in behalf of an institution of the South. That institution is slavery. In like manner, I feel it to be my duty, as a Northern man, to take a counterstand in conversation of one among the dearest of the institutions of the North. This institution is liberty. It is not to assail slavery but to defend liberty that I speak.

It is demanded of us. Do you seek to impose restrictions on Arkansas in violation of the compromise under which Missouri entered the Union? I might content myself with replying that the state of Massachusetts was not a party to that compromise. She never directly or indirectly assented to it. Most of her representatives in Congress voted against it. Those of her representatives who, regarding that compromise in the light of an act of conciliation important to the general interests of the Union, voted for it were disavowed and denounced at home and were stigmatized even here, by a Southern member, as over compliant toward the exactingness of the South.

Let me add in passing, as a kindred fact, which the train of association brings to mind, that it is this very exigency of gentlemen from the South which compels those of the North to act and speak more decidedly than they might be disposed to do of their own mere volition. We come here, generally, imbued with much reluctance to debate the subject of slavery; but whenever it is touched, we hear language addressed to us which necessarily produces revulsion of feeling, a reaction on our part. Our position is changed from that of assailants to the assailed, silence wears the aspect of fear, and concession is converted into pusillanimity. No choice remains to us but to maintain temperately, yet firmly, the rights and the principles of the North. But, continues the gentleman from Virginia, you had no power to impose restrictions upon Missouri; you have no power to impose restrictions upon Arkansas. That was the doctrine of the South then, as the debates of that day abundantly show, and it is now the doctrine of the South.

Sir, I also have looked into the debates and the legislation which preceded the admission of Missouri. Was it without restrictions? The act, which authorized the people of the territory of Missouri to form a constitution and state government, imposed various restrictions upon the powers of the future state, conditional to its admission into the Union, such as the demarcation of its limits, the regulation of public lands within it, and the free navigation of its rivers. The very clause of that statute in which the celebrated compromise consists—the provisions "that in all that territory ceded by France to the United States under the name of Louisiana, which lies north of thirty-six degrees and thirty minutes north latitude, not included within the limits of the state contemplated by this act, slavery and involuntary servitude, otherwise than in the punishment of crimes, whereof the parties shall have been duly convicted, shall be, and is hereby, forever prohibited"—shows that this enactment is in itself an exercise of the right of restriction, both as it regards Missouri and Arkansas, or any other state which may be formed out of the colony of Louisiana. If Congress had a right to prescribe such a restriction for the region north of that parallel of latitude, it had the same right to prescribe it for the region south of that parallel. Although, for reasons satisfactory to itself, it abstained from the exercise of the right in the latter case. Nay, the resolution of the second of March 1821, for the admission of Missouri into the Union, which is now on the table before me, provides that she shall be admitted only "upon the fundamental condition" that a particular clause of her constitution, relating to colored persons, should never take effect. And upon her solemn assent to that condition, and not before, Missouri entered into the Union.

Did not the acts for the admission of Ohio, Indiana, and Illinois impose conditions upon each of those states? Unquestionably. Does not the bill now before us for the admission of Michigan? Ay, and the most onerous one of the relinquishment of a territory which she claims and desires, and the acceptance of another in lieu of it, which she neither claims nor desires.

But, these examples, it may be said, are not precisely in point, since they are drawn from that sacrosanct soil which was dedicated to freedom by Nathan Danes's ordinance. Arkansas stands upon a peculiar footing. It is neither a part of the territory northwest of the Ohio nor of that southwest of the Ohio. It belongs to the territory ceded to us by France. May we exact conditions of the people of that territory, when they ask admission into the Union? That we did so in the case of Missouri, I have already shown. So did we, to a far greater extent, in that of Louisiana. Nay, does not the bill for the admission of Arkansas, as presented to us by its friends, impose restrictions? This very amendment, now under debate, if adopted, will only be one of a series of restrictions.

Our obligation to admit Arkansas into the Union is not created, then, by the terms of the constitution. It is founded on the provisions of the (Louisiana) treaty with France of 1803.

Nor did the people of the colony of Louisiana acquire any privilege, under [the Louisiana Purchase treaty] to exclude Congress from imposing upon them restrictions in favor of liberty on their applying for admission into the Union. It exercised such a power in various important particulars in the case of the state of Louisiana. It exercised it in the case of

Missouri. It exercised it, at the same time, in regard to the rest of the colony, except Arkansas.

In spirit no more can be made of the Missouri Compromise than to say that Arkansas, lying South of the parallel of thirty-six degrees, thirty-nine minutes, shall be admitted on the same conditions with Missouri. This amendment leaves untouched as well the letter as the spirit of the compromise. It does not propose to exclude Arkansas from the Union. It does not require of her to abolish slavery as the condition of her admission into the Union.

This question, I repeat, is a totally different one from that presented and decided in the case of Missouri. There the question was whether Congress would act prohibitively for the abolition of slavery in Missouri. Here the question is whether Congress will act confirmatory for the perpetuation of slavery in Arkansas. Is there a gentleman in this House, not connected personally with the institution of slavery, who can suffer himself to hesitate on such a point?

If Arkansas had been silent on this subject, there might be some plausible pretext for asking us to be silent. But Arkansas having put this noxious matter in her constitution, and having brought it here for our approbation, it is the duty of the members of this House at least to say, "We wash our hands of the unclean thing."

We are engaged in the creation of infant empires. What we shall now do is to act upon generations yet unborn to the end of time. There is no appreciation of the consequences which lie enveloped, like the minute germ of the springing seed, in the work of this hour. And at such a time, shall we, with accents of liberty perpetually on our lips; shall we, whose very institutions are established on the fundamental doctrine of human right; shall we, the representatives of the free people of the United States, be brutishly dumb when it is sought through us to render slavery irredeemably perpetual in a new state soliciting admission into the Union?

I claim it as the right of my constituents, and it is my own right to withhold assent from this exceptionable clause in the constitution of Arkansas.[15]

Against Arkansas's Admission

Representative Hard of New York held that Congress had no power to admit a state into the Union with a constitutional government which authorized and sustained slavery.

In addressing the Committee of the Whole on the night of June 9, 1836, when the bill for the admission of Arkansas was under consideration. Mr. Hard of New York said, in part, the following:

I am unable to perceive any good reason why this important measure should be thus recklessly pushed amidst darkness, fatigue, and confusion, or why gentlemen should be summoned from their beds at this unseasonable hour and compelled to give their voices upon the bill without time or opportunity for examination or reflection. Is it matter of no moment to us or the American people that we are about to add one more state to this Union? Does it afford no rebuke to inconsiderate haste that this bill adds one star more to the constellation or our confederated republic? Do not the safety of the constitution, the defense of civil liberty, and the cause of humanity itself require reflection and consideration before we pass this bill?

We have had no opportunity since the bill was taken up in committee of examining this case. But by the little acquaintance I have obtained with the various matters connected with it, and the few hours' reflection I have bestowed upon the constitution

---

15 *Arkansas Gazette State Centennial Edition,* June 15, 1936.

of Arkansas, I am solemnly impressed with the momentous character of the bill, as a measure vitally connected with the peace of the Union and the harmony and political interests of the nation.

Sir, the decision we make upon this bill will carry with it the interesting result of conferring liberty or perpetuating slavery to millions of human beings yet unborn. Yes, sir, the decision we make this morning, with sleepless eyes and debilitated bodies, will proclaim through your journals to the world and posterity whether the representatives of the people of this far-famed republic, the collected guardians of civil liberty and the rights of man, have the virtue and patriotism to defend and carry out the sound maxims that form the true basis of this excellent form of government; or whether, for the sake of advancing the interest of a miserable partisan policy, they will sacrifice both the honor and liberty of their country by entailing upon the freemen of a sovereign state the interminable institution of slavery.

Sir, we are about to adopt a legislative ordinance which, when sanctioned by the proper authorities, will pass from under our jurisdiction. We can never reclaim it; the faith of the nation will stand pledged to abide by it; and however odious and dangerous it may prove to the harmony of the Union, we can never amend or repeal it. So far as the faith and integrity, if not the power, of Congress are concerned, it will be, like the laws of the Medes and Persians, irrevocably confirmed and established. Is there any circumstance connected with the business of the House to justify for a moment such rashness to legislation? For one, I am not prepared to admit the state of Arkansas on an equal footing with other states, without an effort at least to restrict her to a form of government that shall harmonize with the principles of the constitution. I cannot consent to be driven to sustain a measure fraught with such infinite peril to the cause of personal liberty, without one effort to resist it. I had reason to expect that the committee would have exercised its courtesy in allowing us one day for deliberation. But it has just refused to rise, and has more than intimated its determination by frequent vociferations of question! Question! To push the bill to a passage at this sitting, or at least to place it where they can stop debate by the previous question, I trust I shall be pardoned for detaining it a few moments with a statement of some of the reasons that shall dictate my vote on the bill.

In touching the subject of slavery, or the right claimed by any state to sustain it, I feel all the delicacy and embarrassment anyone can feel, who labors as I do, under a solemn conviction that they are subjects connected with the highest interest, and I may add domestic safety, of the citizens of the South and southwestern states of this Union. And I feel the more painful embarrassment from the fresh recollection of the fearful excitement that pervaded all sections of the country, and the consternation it spread among the slaveholding community, at a period immediately preceding this present session of Congress. I would rather have remained silent than provoked anew those discordant feelings, which, at the early period of our deliberations, had marred the harmony of legislation, and which, though half smothered, still smolders within these walls. I would have refrained from adding one word, but from the impulse of strong sense of paramount duty which I owe to my station, my constituents, and the cause of humanity. Happy would it have been for the country if these subjects could have been deferred until the recent excitement was fully allayed. This excitement has not only threatened a revolution and a separation of the Union, but was fearfully portentous of a servile war, that must have deluged the fairest portion of this country in the blood of our brethren and kindred—a war that would have proved more relentless and implacable to the cries of defenseless innocence that the most terrific wars of the tomahawk and scalping knife.

In submitting my brief remarks, I beg to assure gentlemen of the slaveholding states that while I am opposed to this bill, I hold as sacred and inviolable as anyone in this House the rights secured to all those states who were parties to the original compact. I would as readily engage in a crusade against the Union itself, as touch one word or obliterate one letter of that dear-bought compromise which gave them their rights over their slave property. But, sir, the reasons which impel us to acquiesce in the right to hold human beings in slavery among the original states do by no means authorize Congress to perpetuate it in the new one. There is no compact existing between the general government and any of the new states or the Territory of Arkansas, whereby it has conceded to them the right to barter in human flesh; and I am determined, while I have the honor of a seat on this floor, never to give my vote for a measure that will sanction or permit such a gloomy practice. I shall, therefore, vote very readily and cheerfully against the passage of this bill, and I shall do so under a conscientious belief that Congress has no power to admit a state into the Union with a constitutional government which authorizes and sustains human slavery.

In pursuance of this right and in the exercise of the power, it is the imperious duty of Congress to examine carefully the constitution of Arkansas now before it. And before the state be admitted into the Union, Congress should be satisfied that the constitution under which it intends to organize will secure to the citizens of the state a republican form of government.

On examining the ordinance adopted by the convention of Arkansas, I find, as a whole, it exhibits the most singular incongruity of parts. While it professes to protect liberty, it establishes the most degrading species of slavery and dignifies it with a place in the fundamental charter of the government. It contains many provisions worthy of a free and enlightened people, and such as would excite the admiration of the patriot and philanthropist, while it embraces others that create disgust. It commences, in the language of the convention, with high professions of attachment to the noble maxims of free government and adopts, almost verbatim, the language of the Declaration of Independence. It promises to sustain the personal liberty of the citizen and recommends as essential to the preservation of a free government a diffusion of knowledge and intellectual improvement among the people. In the main, this ordinance asserts and adopts the elementary principles of a republican government; and were it not for the insertion of that odious section in relation to human slavery, that discordant note in the music of its parts, it would have commanded my most cordial approbation.

Does the constitution of Arkansas teach that all men are created equal? That they are endowed with the inalienable right of liberty and the pursuit of happiness? Or does it hold in substance that one part of mankind is born the slaves of the other? That they are esteemed in the light or nature as property, and the unwilling victims of avarice and speculation? Let the ninth article of the constitution of Arkansas answer the question. By that article the slaves of Arkansas are sunk a grade below the brute beasts that herd in your plains or the flocks that feed upon the hills. While it treats the slaves as the personal property of the master, it holds them less protected by the laws of God and man than your beasts of burden.

The important and impending question then properly recurs, whether the letter or the spirit of the federal constitution will authorize Congress to admit to the bosom of our national Union the state of Arkansas, while its constitution or fundamental ordinance embodies political elements hostile to personal liberty and the inalienable rights of its citizens.

By the act of Congress on the sixth of March, 1820, authorizing the people of the Territory of Missouri to form a constitution and state government, there were two very important restrictions imposed upon the convention in relation to this very subject. By the proviso to the fourth section they were required to form a constitution republican in its form, and not repugnant to that of the United States; and by the eighth section, slavery and involuntary servitude were forever prohibited in "all that part of the territory ceded by France to the United States lying north of thirty-six degrees and thirty minutes of north latitude, and not included within the limits of that state." Under this act, the people of Missouri, on the twelfth of June of the same year, called a convention and agreed upon a constitution embracing an article in principle precisely like that in the ninth article of the constitution of Arkansas, prohibiting its general assembly from passing any law emancipating slaves without the consent of the owner. There was another clause in their constitution equally repugnant to civil liberty, which prohibited free Negroes and mulattoes from settling in that state under any pretext whatever. This constitution was submitted to Congress at its next session and gave rise to a discussion which, whether we consider its protracted length or the thrilling interest it excited throughout the country, has never been surpassed on any other occasion in the annals of our legislation. This fearful war of words, which put in jeopardy the Union itself, resulted in the adoption of a resolution by Congress admitting that state into the Union, upon the fundamental condition that the convention should repeal the fourth clause of the twenty-sixth section of the third article in her constitution, which authorizes her legislature to pass laws prohibiting "free Negroes and mulattoes from settling in that state under any pretext whatever," and pledge the faith of the state that no such law ever should be passed. The convention of Missouri assented to the restriction imposed by the resolution and complied with the condition. By a subsequent provision of the general government, she was admitted into the Union without the addition of one word or one syllable in relation to the subject of slavery.

But, sir, if there were a compact or compromise, who were the parties? The Federal Government and sovereignty of Missouri were the parties' litigant, or contracting parties. Admit this to be a compact, and the terms just recited the articles of stipulation, and what connection or relation does it bear to the constitution of Arkansas? What right or power had Missouri to make a compact or compromise which should act, prospectively, over a new, uninhabited, and then surveyed wilderness, wholly without its boundaries? What right had Missouri to dictate terms of admission to a state not then in existence? Surely, if such compromise had been formed, the people of Arkansas would have been at full liberty to disavow it. It could not bind them, neither could the general government. This is not a compromise, not even as it regards Missouri, much less in its operation upon the rights and immunities of the people of Arkansas.

Chapter 8

<u>Statehood and Slavery</u>

The course of the Arkansas statehood bill in Congress was marked by the offering of numerous antislavery petitions, memorials, and remonstrances. Some of these protests made specific objection to the admission of Arkansas with a clause in its constitution that forbade the legislature ever to emancipate slaves without the consent of their owners. Others simply objected to Arkansas's admission as a slave state. (Yet it was not slavery so much as the approaching presidential election, according to Senator Benton of Missouri, that was responsible for opposition in Congress to the admission of Arkansas.)

It was in 1835 that the flood of antislavery petitions, remonstrances, and memorable beggars came pouring into Congress. The National Anti-Slavery Society, which had been organized in Philadelphia as the outgrowth of the New England Anti-Slavery Society formed earlier in Boston, had as its purpose the establishing of subsidiary societies throughout the country to employ agents to spread antislavery sentiment and disseminate literature, and to enlist press and pulpit in the cause. A quantity of antislavery printed matter was seized and burned in Charleston, South Carolina, in the summer of 1835, and President Jackson in his December 1835 message to Congress recommended the passage of a law for the severe penalization of circulating the South any literature intended to stir the slaves to insurrection. The petitions to Congress were, as a rule, for the abolition of slavery in the District of Columbia and the territories, and their multiplicity was such that their presentation sometimes consumed the entire petition period. As the flow increased, H. L. Pinckney of South Carolina on February 8, 1836, moved that they be referred to a select committee. The committee was appointed. It consisted of Pinckney as chairman, Hamer of Ohio, Pierce of New Hampshire, Hardin of Kentucky, Jarvis of Maine, Owens of Georgia, Muhlenberg of Pennsylvania, Dromgoole of Virginia, and Turrill of New York. On May 28, the committee offered a resolution providing that all petitions and papers submitted to the House pertaining to slavery or its abolition, be laid upon the table without being printed or read. The resolution was adopted after a bitter debate by a vote of 117 to 68. This, the first of the so-called "gag" resolutions, was adopted in each succeeding session until the fifth, in 1840, was made a standing rule and remained in effect until it was abandoned in 1844.

On April 11, 1836, Mr. Slade of Vermont presented a memorial from eighty-six citizens of Philadelphia against the admission of Arkansas, with a constitution sanctioning the existence of slavery and prohibiting its abolition. On April 18, Mr. Slade presented the petition of eighty-one citizens of Bristol, Pennsylvania, remonstrating against the admission of Arkansas. On June 6 Mr. Slade presented memorials from 296 males and 52 females of Addison County and its vicinity in the state of Vermont; from 103 citizens of Hanover, 60 males and 44 females of Boscawyn, 59 citizens of Somersworth, and 62 males and 70 females of Concord in the state of New Hampshire; from 39 males and 61 females in the state of Massachusetts; from Guy C. Samson and seven others of Goshen in the state of Rhode Island; and from 37 citizens of Philadelphia and 32 citizens of Adams County in the state of Pennsylvania.

On June 6, 1836, Mr. Pearce of Rhode Island presented a memorial. Mr. Judson of Connecticut presented remonstrance against the admission of Arkansas with slavery in its constitution from citizens of Willimantic, Windham, Plainfield, Woodstock, and Hampton, Connecticut.

On June 6, 1836, John Quincy Adams, the former president of the United States who was then serving as a representative from Massachusetts, presented twenty-two memorials and remonstrance's for citizens of Massachusetts, Pennsylvania, and Ohio, and spoke at length, first to the Committee of the Whole and then in the House.

Henry Clay and Arkansas

From Gales and Seaton's Register of Debates in Congress, April 12, 1836.

Mr. Clay rose to present several petitions which had come into his hands. They were signed by citizens of Philadelphia, many of whom were known to be the first respectability, and the others were no doubt entitles to the highest consideration. The petitions were directed against the admission of Arkansas into the Union while there was a clause in her constitution prohibiting any future legislation for the abolition of slavery within her limits. He had felt considerable doubt as to the proper disposition which he should make of these questions, while he wished to acquit himself of the duty entrusted to him. The bill for the admission of Arkansas had passed the Senate and gone to the other House. It was possible that it would be returned from that branch with an amendment, which would bring this subject into consideration. He wished the petitioners had selected some other organ. He did not concur in the prayer of the petitioners. He thought that Arkansas and any other state or territory south of forty degrees had the entire right, according to the compromise made on the Missouri question, to frame its constitution in reference to slavery as it might think proper. He adhered to the opinions on this point that he held on a former memorable occasion, which would be in the recollection of Senators. He would only ask that one of these memorials be read and that the whole of them should then be laid on the table.

Mr. King of Alabama expressed his regret that the senator from Kentucky had introduced these petitions while a bill was pending in the other branch, in the progress of which it was probable that this question would be stirred. If the presentation of these petitions should bring up again the agitation which was produced by the discussion of the Missouri question, it would be difficult to predict the consequences which might ensure. When the Missouri question was under consideration, he acted with the senator from Kentucky and agreed to give up certain rights of the new states for the purpose of conciliation. But he would now say that never again would he give up anything for the purpose of conciliating another quarter of the country. He repeated his astonishment and concern that the senator from Kentucky should have brought forward the position.

Mr. Clay said he felt unaffected surprise at the expression of regret contained in the language of the senator from Alabama as to the presentation of these petitions. "I," said Mr. Clay, "feel no regret. The subject of these petitions I do not approve, and I stated my disapprobation. I should have been happy had the petitioners chosen another organ. I stated further that my opinions were unchanged. But these petitions have been committed to my care. In presenting them I only performed a duty—a duty in reference to petitions of a constitutional, almost a sacred, character. I have presented the petitions, but I have asked for no other action on them than the mere laying of them on the table, although I might have done so, as the bill is yet before the other branch. It is highly competent to the legislative authority to pass another bill to control this clause in the constitution of Arkansas. I have asked no such thing. If the question should be stirred in the other branch, as seems to be apprehended by the senator from Alabama, it is better that the petitions are presented here. Here they are. I have merely performed a duty in presenting them; yet I am chided, chided at least in tone, by the senator from Alabama for having done so. Sure I am, sir, that in this tone of chiding there is not another senator on this floor who will participate."

The petitions were then laid on the table.

Sharp Criticism of the Action of Henry Clay

Henry Clay's action was the subject of the following comment by a correspondent of the *Arkansas Gazette*, which appeared in the issue of May 17, 1836:

> Washington City, April 12, 1836. From the proceedings of the Senate on yesterday, you will perceive to your astonishment that Henry Clay, the reputed author of the Missouri compromise, upon the question of slavery, has become the mouthpiece and organ of the abolitionist of Philadelphia. Although he disclaims an approval of their prayer, he yet holds out to them encouragement in their efforts to deprive us of our slaves. He talks of an addition act by which their object could be obtained, and presents amendments upon this subject in the House of Representatives, to the bill for our admission and all that. Read his speech; it will speak for itself. He justifies himself upon the ground that he considers it his duty—a duty in reference to petitions of a constitutional, almost sacred, character. Remember, these citizens of Philadelphia are not his constituents, and that the duty he spoke of is calculated to excite the whole country upon the most delicate of all subjects. And further, where was the sanctity of the character of petition when he voted against the president's petition to spread his defense against his famous resolution upon the journals of the Senate? As the old saying is, "The cock won't fight."[16]

Henry Clay, who was born April 12, 1777, in Hanover County, Virginia, a neighborhood known as "the Slashes," removed to Lexington, Kentucky, in 1792. He was self-educated both in the law and in the rhetoric, history, etc., that later brought him fame as an orator. He was successful from the start in law as well as in politics. He advocated

---

16 *Arkansas Gazette*, May 17, 1836.

emancipation for Kentucky before the Constitutional Convention of 1799. Later he was speaker of the Kentucky House and US senator by appointment. He was an elected member of the Senate at his death on June 29, 1852. In the meantime he had served almost continuously for fourteen years as speaker in the lower house of Congress, served as secretary of state under President Quincy Adams, had three times been nominated for the presidency, and had refused cabinet posts under Presidents Madison, Monroe, and Harrison.

Congress and Antislavery Petitions

The resolution adopted in May 1836 was as follows:

"*Resolved,* that Congress possesses no constitutional authority to interfere in any way with the institution of slavery in any of the states of this Confederacy. *Resolved*, that Congress ought not to interfere in any way with slavery in the District of Columbia.

"And whereas it is extremely important and desirable that the agitation of this subject should be finally arrested, for the purpose of restoring tranquility to the public mind, your committee respectfully recommend the adoption of the following additional resolution:

"*Resolved*, that all petitions, memorials, resolutions, prepositions, or papers relating in any way or to any extent whatever to the subject of slavery shall, without being printed or referred, be laid upon the table, and that no further action whatever shall be had thereon."

Protest by John Quincy Adams

Adams was willing that Arkansas be admitted to the Union as a slaveholding state but objected to its Constitution withholding from the legislature power to emancipate slaves without the consent of their owners.

When John Quincy Adams on June 6, 1836, offered his twenty-two petitions and memorials objecting to the admission of Arkansas on account of slavery, Speaker James K. Polk held that, under a resolution adopted by the House, they should be laid on the table.

Mr. Adams spoke at length at the session of June 9. His remarks dealing with the admission of Arkansas, as prepared by Mr. Adams himself for publication in the Gales and Seaton's Register of Debates in Congress were as follows:

On Thursday, the ninth of June, the House went into Committee of the Whole on the state of the Union upon two bills: one to fix the northern boundary of the state of Ohio, and for the conditional admission of the state of Michigan into the Union; and the other for the admission of the state of Arkansas into the Union.

The bill for fixing the northern boundary of the state of Ohio, and the conditional admission of Michigan into the Union, was first taken up for the consideration and gave rise to debates which continued till near one o'clock of the morning of Friday, the tenth of June. Repeated motions to adjourn had been made and rejected. The committee had twice found itself without a quorum and had been thereby compelled to rise and report the fact to the House. In the first instance, there had been found within private calling distance a sufficient number of members, who, though absent from their duty of attendance upon the House, were upon the alert to appear and answer to their names to make a quorum to vote against adjourning, and then to retire again to their amusement or repose. Upon the first restoration of the quorum by this operation, the delegate from Arkansas said that if the committee would only take up and read the bill, he would not urge any discussion upon it then and would consent to the committee's rising and resuming the subject at the next sitting of the House. The bill was accordingly read; a motion was then made for the committee to rise, and it was rejected. An amendment to the bill was moved on taking the question upon which there was no quorum. The usual expedient of private call to straggling members was found ineffectual. A call of the House was ordered at one o'clock in the morning. This operation, to be carried through all its stages, must necessarily consume about three hours of time, during which the House can do no other business. Upon this call, after the names of all the members had been twice called over, and all the absentees for whom any valid or plausible excuse was offered had been excused, there remained eighty-one names of members who, by the rules of the House, were to be taken into custody as they should appear, or were to be sent for and taken into custody where they might be found by special messengers appointed for that purpose. At this hour of the night the city of Washington was ransacked by these special messengers, and the members of the House were summoned from their beds to be brought in custody of these special messengers before the House to answer for their absence. After hearing the excuses of two of these members, and the acknowledged no good reason of a third, they were all excused in a mass without payment of fees; which fees, to the amount of $200 or $300, have of course become a charge upon the people and to be paid with their money.

By this operation, between four and five o'clock of the morning, a small quorum of the House was obtained, and without any vote of the House, the Speaker left the chair, which was resumed by the chairman of the Committee of the Whole. The bill for the admission of Arkansas into the Union was again taken up. The amendment moved before the call of the House was renewed, discussed, and rejected; other amendments were proposed and shared the same fate.

About six o'clock in the morning a motion was made that the committee should rise and report the bills, when Mr. Adams moved an amendment to the eighth section of the bill for the admission of Arkansas. To understand the import and bearing of which, it may be necessary to quote the part of the section into which he proposed its insertion. In the following citation, the words proposed by him for insertion are those enclosed in brackets.

"Section 8. And be it further enacted, that the state of Arkansas is admitted into the Union upon the express condition that the people of the said state shall never interfere with the primary disposal of the public lands within the said state, nor shall they levy a tax on any of the lands of the United States within the said state; and nothing in the this act shall be construed as an assent by Congress [to the article in the constitution of the said state in relation to slavery and the emancipation of slaves, or] to all or any of the propositions contained in the ordinance of the said convention of the people of Arkansas, nor to deprive the said state of Arkansas of the same grants, subject to the same restrictions, which were made to the state of Missouri by virtue of an act entitled an act to authorize the people of the Missouri Territory to form a constitution and state government, and for the admission of such state into the Union on an equal footing with the original states, and to prohibit slavery in certain territories, approved the sixth day of March 1820."

When the amendment had been read by the clerk and the question stated, Mr. Adams addressed the chairman of the committee to the following effect:

Mr. Chairman, on Monday last I had the honor of presenting to this House twenty-two memorials and remonstrances, most of them numerously signed, by citizens of the state of Ohio, of Pennsylvania, and of Massachusetts. Twelve of these memorials were from the congressional district which I represent, from my own constituents, male and female. For in New England and elsewhere, the vote of the men is the vote of the women, and I consider the wives and daughters of the men who vote at my election, whether for me or for any other person, as much my constituents, for all purposed by which I can, as their representative, serve them in this House as if every individual had deposited in the ballot box a vote in my favor.

I was, then, bound in duty to present these memorials and remonstrances to the House; and if that duty was of perfect and irremissible obligation, with regard to those which came from my own immediate constituents, I felt it as not less imperative with regard to those which, proceeding from remoter distances and from persons entirely unknown to me, carried with them a manifestation of confidence reposed in me by the memorials, which it was not less my sacred duty to justify by a grateful return.

I felt it, therefore, my further duty in invite the House to listen to these memorials and remonstrances, to examine their complaints and, so far as might be consistent with the duties of the House to their other constituents and to the nation, to relieve the complainants and to remove the grievance against which they remonstrate.

In the memorials from my own district I recognized among the signatures the names of persons well known to me as citizens, for intelligence, integrity, and benevolence, surpassed by none others in this Union. I had made inquiries concerning the characters of others (of the memorialists) not known to myself and had received testimonials from sources entitled to unqualified credence, and from persons in nowise favoring the purposes of the memorialists; testimonials to their integrity and respectability which could leave in that respect not the shadow of a doubt upon my mind.

The memorials and remonstrances, differing somewhat from one another in their language and phraseology, all complained of one article in the newly formed constitution of Arkansas; and all the remonstrances were against the admission of Arkansas into the Union as a slave state.

The obnoxious article of the constitution of Arkansas is the first section of the second division of the ninth article, and is in the words following:

Emancipation of slaves

"Section 1. The General Assembly shall have no power to pass laws for the emancipation of slaves without the consent of the owners. They shall have no power to prevent emigrants to this state from bringing with them such persons as are deemed slaves by the laws of anyone of the United States. They shall have power to pass laws to permit the owners of slaves to emancipate them, saving the rights of creditors and preventing them from becoming a public charge. They shall have power to prevent slaves from being brought to this state as merchandise, and also to oblige the owners of slaves to treat them with humanity."

Mr. Chairman, I cannot consistently, with my sense of my obligations as a citizen of the United States and bound by oath to support their constitution, object to the admission of Arkansas into the Union as a slave state; I cannot purpose or agree to make it a condition of her admission that a convention of her people shall expunge this article from her constitution. She is entitled to admission as a slave state, as Louisiana and Mississippi, and Alabama, and Missouri have been admitted, by virtue of that article in the treaty for the acquisition of Louisiana, which secures to the inhabitants of the ceded territories all the rights, privileges, and immunities of the original citizens of the United States, and stipulates for their admission, conformably to that principle, into the Union. Louisiana was purchased as a country wherein slavery was the established law of the land. As Congress has not power in time of peace to abolish slavery in the original states of the Union, they are equally destitute of the power in those parts of the territory ceded by France to the United States by the name of Louisiana, where slavery existed at the time of the acquisition. Slavery is in this Union the subject of internal legislation in the states, and in peace is cognizable by Congress only, as it is tacitly tolerated and protected where it exists by the Constitution of the United States, and as it mingles in their intercourse with other nations. Arkansas, therefore, comes, and has the right to come, into the Union with her slaves and her slave laws. It is written in the bond, and however I may lament that it ever was so written, I must faithfully perform its obligations.

I could not, therefore, propose or support the specific measure desired by the memorialists, which was to impose a restriction upon the people of the state of Arkansas, by requiring of them, as a condition of their admission into the Union, that they should expunge from their constitution the article concerning slavery. I did not think it within the legitimate powers of Congress, under the present existing circumstances, to impose upon the state of Arkansas any restriction whatever, with relation to slavery, in the formation of her constitution. Upon the same principle, I had been opposed to the proposal of restriction upon the state of Missouri question; for there were two Missouri questions, differing much from each other, and which were debated at two successive sessions of Congress. The second was that finally adjusted by the compromise. The first was that in which the restriction was proposed, and my opinion had at the time been freely expressed against it.

But then I disapproved, as I now disapprove, of slavery as a civil institution. As a citizen, and as a man, therefore, I disapprove of that article in the constitution of Arkansas, the object of which is to perpetuate slavery. In voting for the acceptance of that constitution, and for the admission of the State into the Union, I do not hold myself bound to approve of all its internal regulations; but doctrines have been recently broached and are now countenanced by the transfer of the lawful possessions of Michigan to the state of Ohio, which make it, in my judgment, proper, and perhaps necessary, that Congress, the representatives of that federation, compounded partly of slaveholding and partly of entirely free states, should disclaim all approbation of, or assent to, that article in the constitution of Arkansas. I propose no restriction upon her. I am content to receive her as one of the slaveholding states of this Union; but I am unwilling that Congress, in accepting her constitution, should even lie under the imputation of assenting to the article in the constitution of a state which withholds from its legislature the power of giving freedom to the slave.

In this very section of the bill now before the committee, Congress refuses their assent to propositions, made by the convention of the people of Arkansas which formed their constitution, and were transmitted with it. My proposed amendment, very short and simple, is in perfect accordance and keeping with the remainder of the section, as it stands in the bill now before the committee; and although I cannot flatter myself that it will be satisfactory to those of my constituents and fellow citizens who have thought proper to commit their memorials and remonstrance's to me, it will at least secure to me the consciousness of having discharged my duty to them, to my country, and to that reverence for the rights of mankind, which rejects, without reserve, the principle that, by the law of nature or of God, man can be the property of man.

Upon this topic I will not enlarge. Were I disposed so, to dim twenty hours of continuous session have too much exhausted my own physical strength, and the faculties as well as the indulgence of those who might incline to hear me, for me to trespass longer upon their patience. When the bill shall be reported to the House, I may, perhaps, again ask to be heard upon renewing there, as I intend, the motion for this amendment.

Mr. Adams resumed his seat, and Mr. Wise addressed the committee. The debate was continued by Mr. Briggs, Mr. Cushing, Mr. Hoar, and Mr. Hard of New York, and by Mr. Wise in reply, particularly, to Mr. Cushing. There was great disorder and confusion in the hall, occasioned chiefly by calls for order and vociferations of the word "question." Personal reflections passed between two Southern gentlemen, which were, however, finally adjusted without bloodshed. The chairman of the committee, with great and indefatigable exertions, succeeded so far in restoring order that Mr. Hoar was heard with respectful attention. After he took his seat, as the question was about to be put, Mr. Adams addressed the committee to the following import:

Mr. Chairman, it was not my intention to have troubled the committee with another word upon the subject of my proposed amendment. But the gentleman from Virginia (Mr. Wise) has been pleased to propound to me a number of direct questions, two or three of which I heard, and to them I am willing to give direct and explicit answers. For however widely I differ in opinion from him on this and most other occasions of common deliberation in this hall, I will do him the justice which he has done me and say that there is nothing of indirection or ambiguous giving out in him. His course is straight forward, and you may always know where to find him. And, sir, in the intercourse of public or private life, I hold in higher esteem an adversary of such a character than the political vane upon the steeple, whose friendship and whose opinions swing round the compass with every irritation of the winds and are steadfast only to the breath of the breeze.

One of the gentleman's questions which I heard was, "From whence this amendment came?" I answer him directly that it came from me and from me alone, without consultation with any other human being. There was no abolition gunpowder plot in it; but in claiming it as all my own, I shall not record a specification of it in the Patent Office as for an ingenious invention or a profound discovery. It laid in my way, and I took it up. A respectable portion of my constituents and many others of my fellow citizens had charged me with the duty of presenting their memorials against the slavery article in the constitution of Arkansas. Multitudes of others had entrusted to me their petitions for the abolition of slavery and the slave trade in the District of Columbia. Great numbers of petitions, memorials, and remonstrances of the same purport had been presented by my colleagues and by other members of the House. I had been earnestly solicited to support, as far as my very slender influence in this House might extend and as far as my own convictions of truth and justice would admit, the prayer of those petitions and the purpose of those remonstrances and memorials. I could not support the immediate abolition of slavery in the District of Columbia. I could not resist the admission of Arkansas, notwithstanding the slavery article in her constitution, into the Union. But there was a point of concession to the slaveholding interests of the South, from the representatives of none but freemen in the House, where it appeared to me not only just, but indispensably necessary, to stop.

Slavery, taking advantage of political influences, operated just at this time at the North upon the prospects of the presidential election—taking advantage (I must say no very generous advantage) of that kind, friendly, and compassionate feeling of Northern freemen for their brethren and fellow citizens, the slaveholders of the South, who during the last twelve months had universally pervaded the Northern region of the country and urged our people sometimes even to riotous excess against the peaceable, warmhearted but honest-hearted enthusiasts of human liberty. Slavery, I say in the confidence of her temporary reinforcement from sources foreign to her own character, had changed her tone and was aiming blows of deadly intent at the freedom of her Northern associate itself. She had struck at the freedom of the press and at the freedom of the post office, both in this and other branches of the legislature, and by the express recommendation of the chief magistrate of the Union; she had struck at the liberty and the life of a free citizen of a Northern state by demanding that he should be delivered up innocent of all offence, as he was, against the laws of the state in which he dwelt, to the tender mercies of her felony, without benefit of clergy. I had seen the twenty-two memorials and remonstrance's which I had presented, and my other of the same import, the moment they had reached the hands of the clerk, ordered by the speaker to be laid on the table, without reading, without the privilege of being considered by a general stigmatizing interdict, more insulting than would have been an absolute refusal to receive them. The article in the constitution of Arkansas, cutting off the last hope of emancipation to the end of time by withholding from the legislature even the power of ordaining it, I strongly disapproved. The House had treated all these memorials and remonstrances in behalf of freedom as if they were afraid to hear them read, afraid to look them in the face, afraid even to squint at them. In reading this eighth section of the bill before the committee, it appeared to me that the amendment which I offered was so congenial to its spirit that, if inserted at the place proposed, it would appear altogether as if it had been a part of the section as originally drawn up. The amendment falls infinitely short of the Missouri restriction, and it is entirely congenial to the spirit of the constitution itself. Unable as I was to propose the restriction desired by the memorialists and remonstrances, yet, believing that the occasion required of me an avowal of those opinions and principles, the only guardians of the freedom of my constituents, I was desirous of manifesting them in the form the least offensive possible to the slaveholding port of the community. I wished to plant the standard of freedom at the very lowest point of its elevation, and by conceding to slavery everything required by the common compact, yet adhering to those self-evident truths proclaimed in the declaration of the independence, to utter the minimum of the sentiments which I believed my constituents would never resign but with the last drop of their blood. At every former period of our history, I should have expected that the representatives of the slaveholding states in this House would readily have accepted this as far more favorable to them then the Missouri compromise. Now my object is to fulfill the duty devolved upon me by my constituents and leave the decision where it properly belongs. I am not aware of any other question of the gentleman from Virginia which requires an answer from me, particularly after the eloquent address of my colleague behind me (Mr. Cushing) has already answered them so much more effectually than I could have done myself.

Mr. Wise rose and inquired whether in the opinion of the gentleman from Massachusetts (Mr. Adams), if his amendment should prevail, the state of Arkansas would, by this bill, be admitted in the Union.

Mr. Adams: Certainly, sir. There is not in my amendment the shadow of a restriction upon the state. It leaves the state, like all the rest, to regulate the subject of slavery within herself to her own laws; and how far that comes short of the concessions required from the slaveholding interest by the Missouri compromise, it is easy to judge by reference to the transactions of that time. For in the act of the sixth of March, 1820, to authorize the people of the Missouri Territory to form a constitution and state government, and for the admission of that state into the Union, slavery was and is forever prohibited in all the territory ceded by France to the United States under the name of Louisiana, which lies north of thirty-six degrees and thirty minutes of north latitude, not included within the limits of the state of Missouri compromise; not the abolition, but the prohibition by Congress, forever, of slavery in that portion of the Louisiana Territory where it had not then penetrated. And, secondly, when the constitution of the state of Missouri was formed, there was an article on the legislative power, the fourth clause of the twenty-sixth powers and duties of the general assembly of the state was in these words: "It shall be their duty, as soon as may be, to pass such laws as may be necessary, first, to prevent free Negroes and mulattoes from coming to and settling in this state under any pretext whatsoever."[17]

John Quincy Adams

John Quincy Adams, the sixth president of the United States, had been minister to three European countries, US senator from Massachusetts, and secretary of state of the United States before his election to the presidency; he became a member of the national House of Representatives afterward. He was born in Quincy, Massachusetts, on July 11, 1767, son of John Adams, the second president. He was abroad on diplomatic service during his youth, and though he graduated from Harvard University later, he received most of his early education

---

[17] *Register of Debates in Congress,* Washington, DC: Gales & Seaton, 1837.

in Paris, Amsterdam, and Leipsic. At the age of fourteen, he served as secretary to Francis Dana, envoy to Russia, and sixteen years later he was appointed minister to that country. Before then he had served as minister resident at the Hague, and it was after his service in the United States that he became minister to Great Britain, serving two years and returning to the United States in 1817 to become secretary of state under President Monroe. At the close of Monroe's term, Adams was put forward as a candidate for the presidency. When the electoral college was unable to decide between General Jackson, Mr. Adams, William H. Crawford, and Henry Clay, the election was thrown into the House of Representatives, where, with Clay's influence going to Adams, he was named. He was defeated for the ensuing term by Jackson in 1828, and though he desired to retire to private life, his friends persuaded him to become a candidate to represent his Massachusetts districts in Congress. He was elected in 1830 and held the office until his death in Washington on February 23, 1848.

Chapter 9

Statehood and Politics

Vote for Martin Van Buren for president.

At the time the Arkansas statehood bill was pending in Congress, Martin Van Buren, the chosen political heir of President Andrew Jackson, had been nominated for president by the Democratic Party. (Then called the Republican Party.) Hugh Lawson White of Tennessee, who had been formally closely attached to Andrew Jackson, was favored for president by those Democrats who were opposed to Jackson. The fact that White was a Tennessean was expected to embarrass Jackson in his support of the New Yorker Van Buren. The Whigs, with whom White had voted on some important legislation, for a while talked of nominating him as their candidate. White, who was called "the Cato of the Senate," was known for his high character, his sound sense, and his faithful devotion to duty. William Henry Harrison was the Whig candidate. Massachusetts, however, gave its electoral vote to Daniel Webster. South Carolina voted for Senator Willie Mangum of North Carolina. White carried only Tennessee and Georgia. He disappointed the Whig hope that he would win enough Democratic states to throw the presidential contest into the House of Representatives. Harrison got 73 electoral votes by carrying Delaware, Indiana, Kentucky, Maryland, New Jersey, Ohio, and Vermont. Van Buren carried Connecticut, Maine, New Hampshire, Rhode Island, Alabama, Arkansas, Louisiana, Mississippi, Missouri, North Carolina, Virginia, Illinois, Michigan, Pennsylvania, and New York. With 170 electoral votes Van Buren had a majority of 46, but he failed to carry all the states Jackson had carried, and the Democratic majority in the House was reduced to two over the Whigs, with 10 independent members holding the balance of power.

Thomas H. Benton's Account

In his *Thirty Year's View*, a work considered of great value for the history of the period with which it deals, Thomas Hart Benton, senator from Missouri from 1820 to 1850, devotes a chapter to the admission of Arkansas and Michigan to the Union.

"I was in the Senate," he says by the way of preface, "the whole time of which I write—an active business member, attending and attentive—in the confidence of half the administrations, and a close observer of the others—had an inside view of transactions of which the public only saw the outside, and of many of which the two sides were very different—saw the secret springs and hidden machinery by which men and parties were to be moved, and measures promoted or thwarted—saw patriotism and ambition at their respective labors and was generally able to discriminate between them."

In writing of the admission of Arkansas and Michigan, Senator Benton said,

> These two young States had applied to Congress for an act to enable them to hold a convention and form state constitutions, preparatory to admission into the Union. Congress refused to pass the acts, and the people of the two territories held the convention by their own authority, formed their constitutions—sent copies to Congress, praying admission as states. They both applied at this session, and the proceedings on their respective applications were simultaneous in Congress, though in separate bills. That of Michigan was taken up first and had been brought before each House in a message from the resident.
>
> The bill passed the Senate by rather a close vote—twenty-four to eighteen; the latter being all senators in the opposition. It then went to the House of Representatives for concurrence.

From the time of the admission of new states, it had been the practice to admit a free and slave state alternately, so as to keep up a numerical equilibrium between them—a practice resulting from some slight jealousy existing, from the beginning, between the two classes of states. In 1820, when the Missouri controversy inflamed that jealousy, the state of Massachusetts divided herself to furnish territory for the formation of a new free state (Maine) to balance Missouri; and the acts of Congress for the admission of both were passed contemporaneously in March 1820. Now, in 1836, when the slave question again was much inflamed, and a state of each kind to be admitted, the proceedings for that purpose were kept as nearly together as possible, not to include them in the same bill. The moment, then, that the Michigan bill had passed the Senate, that of Arkansas was taken up, under the lead of Mr. Buchanan, to whom the Arkansas application had been confided, as that of Michigan had been to Mr. Benton. This latter senator alluded to this circumstance to show that the people of these young states had no fear of trusting their rights and interests to the care of senators differing from themselves on the slavery question.[18]

Six Votes Against Arkansas

Mr. Alexander Porter of Louisiana would vote against the admission, on account of the "revolutionary" proceedings of the people in the formation of their constitution without a previous act of Congress. It is believed that Mr. Clay voted upon the same ground. There were but six votes against the admission, namely Mr. Clay, Mr. Knight of Rhode Island, Mr. Porter, Mr. Prentiss, Mr. Robbins of Rhode Island, and Mr. Swift. It is believed that Mr. Robbins and Mr. Knight voted on the same ground with Mr. Clay and Mr. Porter. The two bills were

---

18 Thomas Benton, *Thirty Years' View,* New York: D. Appleton and Co., 1883.

made the special order (in the House) for the same day, Wednesday, the eighth of June, Congress being to adjourn on the Fourth of July; and the Michigan bill having priority on the calendar, as it had first passed the Senate.

After Mr. Wise of Virginia moved to postpone the Michigan bill until the following Monday, Mr. Thomas of Maryland objected.

These latter words of Mr. Thomas (that friends of Arkansas could stop the Michigan bill at any time until satisfied that the Missouri compromise was not to be disregarded) revealed the point of jealousy between some Southern and Northern members and brought the observance of the Missouri compromise fully into view as a question to be tried.

Mr. Lewis of North Carolina took decided ground in favor of giving the Arkansas bill the priority of decision and expressed himself thus: "He should vote for the proposition of the gentleman from Virginia (Mr. Wise) to lay the bill for the admission of Michigan into the Union on the table, until the bill for the admission of Arkansas should be first passed. He should do this, for the obvious reason that there were dangers, he would not say how great, which beset Arkansas, and which did not beset Michigan. The question of slavery could be moved as a condition for the admission of Arkansas, and it could not as a condition for the admission of Michigan. I look upon the Arkansas question as therefore the weaker of the two, and for that reason I would give it precedence. Besides, upon the delicate question which may be involved in the admission of Arkansas, we may be the weaker party in this House. For that reason, if gentlemen mean to offer no obstructions to the admission of Arkansas, let them give the assurance by helping the weaker party through with the weaker question. The gentleman from Pennsylvania (Mr. Sutherland) says that these two bills will be hostages for the safety of each other. No, sir, if you pass the stronger bill in advance of the weaker. Besides, the North wants no hostages on this subject. Their institutions cannot be attacked. We of the South want a hostage to protect us on a delicate question; and the effect of giving precedence to the Michigan bill is to deprive us of that hostage."

The Arkansas bill was ordered to a third reading by a vote of 143 to 50. Here again the beginning and the ending of the list of voters is remarkable, beginning again with Mr. Adams and terminating with Mr. Lewis Williams of North Carolina—two gentlemen wide apart in their political courses and certainly voting on this occasion on different principles.

Significance of the Vote

From the meagerness of these negative votes, it is evident that the struggle was not to pass the two bills but to bring them to a vote. This was the secret of the arduous session of twenty-five hours in the House. Besides the public objections which clogged their admission— boundaries in one, slavery in the other, alien voting, and (what was deemed by some) revolutionary conduct in both in holding conventions without authority of Congress—there was another cause operating silently, and which went more to the postponement than to the rejection of the states. This cause was political and partisan and grew out of the impeding presidential election, to be held before Congress should meet again. Mr. Van Buren was the Democratic candidate; Gen. William Henry Harrison was the candidate of the opposition; and Mr. Hugh L. White of Tennessee was brought forward by a fraction that divided the Democratic Party. The new states, it was known, would vote, if now admitted, for Mr. Van Buren; and this furnished a reason to the friends of the other candidates (even those friendly to eventual admission, and on which some of them were believed to act) to wish to stave off the admission to the ensuing session. The actual negative vote to the admission of each state was not only small but nearly the same in number, and it mixed both as to political parties and sectional localities, so as to exclude the idea of any regular or considerable opposition to

Arkansas as a slave state. The vote which would come nearest to referring itself to that cause was the one on Mr. Adams's proposed amendment to the state constitution; and there the whole vote amounted only to thirty-two. Of the sentiments of the greater part of these, including Mr. Adams himself, the speech of that gentleman must be considered the authentic exponent and will refer their opposition, not to any objection to the admission of the state as slaveholding, but to an unwillingness to appear upon the record as assenting to a constitution which forbids emancipation and made slavery perpetual. The number actually voting to reject the state and keep her out of the Union, because she admitted slavery, must have been quite small—not more in proportion, probably, than what it was in the Senate.

Lines as Drawn in Senate

It was the friends of Jackson's administration and of Van Buren and Johnson against "Clay, Calhoun, & Co." and Hugh Lawson White.

April 26, 1836, *Arkansas Gazette*

From the proceedings of the Senate, which we publish today, it will be seen, that we are solely indebted to the friends of the administration and of Messrs. Van Buren and Johnson,[19] for the passage of the bill for our admission through that body—and that Judge White (Senator Hugh Lawson White of Tennessee) voted against us, and with Clay, Calhoun, & Co., on every party vote that was taken. His voting for Arkansas, on the final passage of the bill for her admission, entitles him to no thanks from her citizens, as he had previously left no effort untried to prevent the passage of the bill for the admission of Michigan, on the passage of which depended the success of our application for

---

19 Richard Mentor Johnson was born near Louisville, Kentucky, on October 17, 1780. He represented his district in the House of Representatives from 1807 to 1819, was United Stated senator from 1819 to 1829, and was later reelected to the House, serving until his election to the vice presidency in 1836. He was a candidate for the vice presidency in 1840 but was defeated.

admission. If she had been rejected, Arkansas would have shared the same fate. These facts ought to be borne in mind by the people of Arkansas and not forgotten when we give our suffrages, next autumn, for electors of president and vice president. If there are any who can give their votes for Judge White, after such a glaring evidence of his bitter hostility to the best interests of Arkansas, they ought to be considered as her worst enemies.

Van Buren's Friends Stood Firm for the Arkansas Bill

The *Arkansas Gazette* published on April 26 the following from a correspondent who was present during the discussion of the Arkansas statehood bill in the Senate.

April 14, 1836, Helena

Dear Sir, I have just returned from Washington City and have the pleasure to announce that I was present in the Senate of United States when the bill admitting Arkansas into the Union passed. The opponents of the administration were indefatigable in using every exertion, both indirectly and directly, to defeat the bill. They strenuously opposed Michigan, and with the vain hope of defeating Arkansas through her. The bill admitting Michigan passed the Senate first, to which bill, just and equitable in all its provisions, I never, in any legislative body, witnessed a more violent and vindictive opposition. They moved adjournment after adjournment—they moved amendment after amendment—but the friends of Mr. Van Buren stood firm and presented to them an unbroken front. The result terminated gloriously and triumphantly. Judge White bent himself, with all the powers he possessed to the opposition, to defeat the just and legitimate rights of the people of Michigan; but truth was omnipotent, and public justice prevailed. Immediately after the bill passed admitting Michigan, Mr. Buchanan called up the bill, previously reported, to admit Arkansas.

The opposition tried to rally again. Clay and Crittenden[20] led the way. They denounced the proceedings of Arkansas as revolutionary and rebellious. They said that the new states of Michigan and Arkansas were monsters—that their births into the Union were forced and premature, and would be tainted with the principles of this administration—that they were hurried into the Union, so as to promote Mr. Van Buren's interest. Honorable Senators these, indeed! Willing to deprive us of our just and equal right, because they fear that we, in the exercise of our political privileges, may support the man of our choice. Judge White voted for Arkansas upon the final passage of the bill. But why? Michigan had passed into the Union as a nonslaveholding state. To defeat Arkansas would have thrown the balance of power into the hands of nonslaveholding states. Judge White, being a representative of a slave state, was compelled, in self-defense, to vote for Arkansas. His alliance with the opponents of General Jackson's administration certainly lays us under no deep obligations to support his claims to the presidency! I do hope, sir, that there will not be a man in Arkansas, so recreant to his interest, as to support the man who is willing to deprive us of equal political privileges with the people of other states. But for the firmness of Mr. Van Buren's friends we should have been defeated.

---

20 John Jordan Crittenden was born near Versailles, Kentucky, on September 10, 1787. He graduated from William and Mary College in 1806, was appointed attorney general of Illinois Territory in 1809, and served in the War of 1812. After serving in the Kentucky legislature, he was elected US senator, taking office in 1817 and resigning in 1819. He was again elected and was in the US Senate from 1835 to 1841. He was then appointed attorney general in the Harrison cabinet but served only from March 5, 1841, to September 13 of the same year. He was then appointed US senator to fill a vacancy caused by the resignation of Henry Clay and was later elected and was in the Senate from 1842 until his resignation in 1848. In 1848, he was elected governor of Kentucky and resigned that office in 1852. He was appointed attorney general in the Fillmore cabinet and served from 1850 to 1853. He was again elected to the US Senate (1855–1861) and as a Unionist to the Thirty-Seventh Congress (1861–1863). He died in Frankfort, Kentucky, on July 26, 1863.

Arkansas Accepts Compact

After Ambrose H. Sevier, Arkansas's delegate in Congress, had seen the constitution and ordinance adopted by the Constitutional Convention, he wrote to the *Arkansas Gazette*, under the date of March 8, 1836, that a "pruning knife would have to be used with heavy hand on the ordinance or it would not go through."

Comparison between the propositions submitted to Congress by the Arkansas convention and the propositions offered in return to Arkansas by Congress will show how heavily the Arkansas ordinance was "pruned." (The ordinance adopted by the Constitutional Convention and the compact adopted by the Congress are published on the following page.)

Sevier said, however, in a letter under date of June 16, 1836: "In our bill, in addition to the provisions granted to Missouri and the new states, we have five sections of land to complete our statehouse. The legislature is to have the disposal of it, and with this exception it is a copy of the Ten Section bill. Michigan and Arkansas have got clear of an iniquitous and ungenerous restriction, which has been invariably imposed upon all the other new states; that is, they are authorized to tax land as soon as sold. In the other states no tax can be imposed upon land for five years after the sale."

Action of Legislature on Articles of Compact

Tuesday, September 13, 1836, Arkansas General Assembly, House of Representatives

Messrs. Tully, Tolleson, May, Hoge, and Taylor were appointed a committee to examine the Act of Congress supplementary to the act for the admission of Arkansas, and also the articles of compact between the United States and state of Arkansas, and report what legislative action is needed thereon.

Monday, September 19, 1836, House of Representatives

Mr. Tully, from the Select Committee to whom the subject was referred, submitted the following report:

Mr. Speaker: The Select Committee appointed to examine the act of Congress "supplementary to the act entitled 'An act for the admission of the state of Arkansas into the Union, and to provide for the due execution of the laws of the United States within the same, and for the other purposes,'" beg leave to submit the following report:

They find that, by an act of the Congress of the United States, approved June fifteenth, one thousand eight hundred and thirty-six, that the state of Arkansas is thereby declared to be one of the United States of America and admitted into the Union on an equal footing with the original states in all respects whatever, according to the boundaries therein designated.

Further, it is declared, in the eighth section of the said act, that nothing in said act shall be construed as an assent, by Congress, to all or any of the propositions contained in the ordinance of the convention of the people of Arkansas. It is also set forth and declared, in the eighth section of the said act, that the state of Arkansas shall be entitled to the "same grants, subject to the same restrictions, which were made to the state of Missouri by virtue of an act entitled 'An act to authorize the people of the Missouri Territory to form a Constitution and State Government, and for admissions of such state into the Union,'" etc., which grants and restrictions are fully set forth in the aforementioned act entitled "An act supplementary to the act entitled 'An act for the admission of the state of Arkansas into the Union.'"

The committee further report that it is expedient that this general assembly accede to and accept the propositions set forth in the above act, and recommend the adoption of the following ordinance: Be it ordained, by the Senate and House of Representatives of the state of Arkansas, that the propositions set forth in an act entitled "An act supplementary to the act entitled 'An act for the admission of the state of Arkansas into the Union, and to provide for the due execution of the laws of the United States within the same, and for other purposes,'" be, and the same are hereby, freely accepted, ratified, and irrevocably confirmed, as articles of compact and union between the state of Arkansas and the United States.

And be it further ordained by the authority aforesaid, that the General Assembly of the state of Arkansas shall never interfere, without the consent of the United States, with the primary disposal of the soil within said state, owned by the United States, nor with any regulations Congress may find necessary for securing the title in such soil to the bona fide purchasers thereof. No tax shall be imposed on lands that are the property of the United States, and in no case shall nonresident proprietors be taxed higher than resident, and that the bounty lands granted, or hereafter to be granted, for military services during that late war, shall, while they continue to be held, by the patentees or their heirs, remain exempt from any tax laid by order, or under the authority of the state, whether for state, county, township or any other purpose, for the term of three years, from and after the date of the patents, respectively.

Mr. Phillips moved that it be laid on the table until Thursday next, which was negative; and then, on motion of Mr. Caldwell, the report was ordered to be printed.

————

Friday, September 23, 1836, Arkansas General Assembly, House of Representatives

On the motion of Mr. Tully, the report of the Select Committee on the ordinance, or articles of compact, submitted by the Congress of the United States to the state of Arkansas, for acceptance of rejection, was then taken up and unanimously adopted.

Saturday, October 8, 1836, Arkansas General Assembly, Senate

The ordinance, accepting, ratifying, and irrevocably confirming the propositions set forth in an act of Congress supplementary to the act for the admission of the state of Arkansas into the Union, was considered in the Committee of the Whole and reported with amendments which were agreed to when the bill was read a third time and passed and returned to the House of Representatives. (On Saturday, October 1, the ordinance had been read a first time and ordered to second reading.)

What Arkansas Submitted and What Congress Offered

The ordinance as proposed by the Constitutional Convention of 1836:

Be it ordained by the convention assembled to form a constitution and system of government for the people of the state of Arkansas, on behalf and by the authority of the people of the said state, the following propositions be submitted to the Congress of the United States, which, if assented to by that body, shall be obligatory and binding on the state of Arkansas:

Section 1. Section No. 16, in every township of public lands, and where such section has been sold, or otherwise disposed of, or unfit for cultivation, other lands equivalent thereto, and as contiguous as may be, shall be granted to the state for the use of schools; a quantity of land equal to two sections, for each and every county, to be located under the direction of the general assembly of the state, according to any of the legal subdivisions of the public lands, shall be granted to the state, for the erection of an academy in each county in the state.

Section 2. All salt springs within the state, and one entire township of the public lands including the same, shall be granted to the state for the use thereof, and the same to be used and deposed of, under such terms, conditions, and regulations as the general assembly shall direct.

Section 3. The hot springs in said state, together with four sections of lands including the said springs, as near the center as may be, shall be granted to the state, for the use thereof, and the same to be disposed of in such manner as the general assembly shall direct.

Section 4. The seventy-two sections of land heretofore granted by the United States, and reserved, or to be reserved by the Secretary of Treasury for the use of a seminary of learning, shall be vested in the General Assembly of the state and appropriated by said general assembly for a seminary or seminaries of learning, as the public good may require.

Section 5. Five per centum of the net proceeds of the sale of public lands lying within said state, and which shall be sold by the United States, from and after the first day of April, one thousand eight hundred and thirty-six, after deducting all expenses incident to the same, shall be reserved for the purposes following, to wit: four-fifths to be disbursed within the state under the direction of the general assembly of the state, for roads and canals, and one-fifth for the encouragement of learning.

Section 6. A quantity of land equal to one township, to be located under the direction of the General Assembly of the state, according to any of the legal subdivisions of the public lands, shall be granted to said state to be applied to the erection or completion of the statehouse and other public buildings, as, in the discretion of the general assembly, as the public good may require.

Section 7. Eight hundred sections of inappropriate public lands lying within this state shall be designated under the direction of the general assembly, and granted to the state, for the purposes of internal improvements.

Section 8. All that section of country lying west of the western boundary of the state of Arkansas, which was formerly a part of the Territory of Arkansas, under the provisions of an act of Congress, approved the twenty-sixth of May, eighteen hundred and twenty-four, entitled, and act to fix the western boundary line of the Territory of Arkansas, and which was ceded by the United States to the Cherokee and Choctaw Indians, whenever the Indian title shall be extinguished to the same, shall be attached to and from a part of the state of Arkansas; and when the said Indian title shall be extinguished, the western boundary of the said state shall be in accordance with the provisions of the said act of the Congress.

Section 9. The people of the state of Arkansas shall never interfere with the primary disposal of the public lands of the United States within the said state, nor shall they levy a tax on any of the lands of the United States within the said state.

Section 10. The roads commenced in this state, for the construction of which appropriations have been made by Congress, shall be completed and put in repair at the expense of the United States.

Section 11. All the public lands within the state of Arkansas which have been offered for sale five years and upward, the title of which is in the United States, shall be granted to the state of Arkansas for such purposes as the general assembly may deem proper.

Section 12. The delegate in Congress from the Territory of Arkansas is hereby authorized and empowered to make or assent to such other propositions, herein made, as the interests of the state may require: and any such changes or new propositions, when approved by the general assembly, shall be as obligatory as if the assent of this convention were given thereto. And all stipulations entered into by the general assembly with the United States, shall be articles of compact between the United States and the state of Arkansas.

Compact (Act of Congress, approved by President Jackson June 23, 1836)

An act supplementary to the act entitled "An act for the admission of the state of Arkansas into the Union, and to provide for the due execution of the laws of the United States within the same, and for other purposed."

Be it enacted by the Senate and House of Representatives of the United States of America in Congress assembled. That in lieu of the proposition submitted to the Congress of the United States, by an ordinance passed by the convention of delegates at Little Rock, assembled for the purpose of making a constitution for the state of Arkansas, which are hereby rejected; and that the following propositions be, and the same are, herby offered to the General Assembly of the state of Arkansas for their free acceptance or rejection; which, if accepted, under the authority granted to the general assembly for this purpose by the convention which framed the Constitution of said state shall be obligatory upon the United States:

First: That the section numbered sixteen in every township, and when such section has been sold or otherwise disposed of, other lands equivalent thereto, and as contiguous as may be, shall be granted to the state for the use of the inhabitants of such townships for the use of schools (a).

Second: That all salt springs, not exceeding twelve in number, with six sections of land adjoining to each, shall be granted to the said state for the use of the said state, the same to be selected by the general assembly thereof on or before the first day of January, one thousand eight hundred and forty; and the same, when so selected, to be used under such terms, conditions, and regulations as the general assembly of the said state shall direct. Provided that no salt spring the right whereof is now vested in any individual or individuals, or which may hereafter be confirmed or adjusted to any individual or individuals, shall by this section, be granted to said state. And provided also that the general assembly shall never sell or lease the same, at any one time, for a longer period than ten years, without the consent of Congress; and that nothing contained in the act of Congress entitled "An act authorizing the governor of the Territory of Arkansas to lease the salt springs in said territory, and for other purposed," or in any other act, shall be construed to give to the said state any further or other claim whatsoever to any salt springs, or lands adjoining thereto, than those hereby granted (b).

Third: That 5 percent of the net proceeds of the sale of the lands lying within the said state, and which shall be sold by Congress from and after the first day of July next, after deducting all expenses incident to the same, shall be reserved for making public roads and canals within the said state, under the direction of the general assembly thereof.

Fourth: That a quantity of land, not exceeding five sections, be, and the same is, hereby granted to the said state in addition to the ten sections which have already been granted for the purpose of completing the public buildings of the said state at Little Rock: which said five sections shall, under the direction of the general assembly of said state, be located, at any time, in legal divisions of not less than one-quarter section, in such townships and ranges as the general assembly aforesaid may select on any of the appropriated lands of the United States within the said state.

Fifth: That the two entire townships of land which have already been located by virtue of the act entitled "An act concerning a seminary of learning in the Territory of Arkansas," approved the second of March, one thousand eight hundred and twenty-seven, are hereby vested in and confirmed to the general assembly of the said state, to be appropriated solely to the use of such seminary by the general assembly (c). Provided that the five foregoing propositions, herein offered, are on the condition that the general assembly or legislature of the said state, by virtue of the powers conferred upon it by the convention which framed the Constitution of the said state, shall provide, by an ordinance irrevocable without the consent of the United States, that the said general assembly of the said State shall never interfere with the primary disposal of the soil within the same by the United States, nor with any regulations Congress may find necessary for securing the title in such soil to the bona fide purchasers thereof; and that no tax shall be imposed on lands the property of the United States; and that in no case shall nonresident proprietors be taxed higher than residents; and that the bounty lands granted, or hereafter to be granted, for military services during the late war, shall, while they continue to be held by the patentees or their heirs, remain exempt from any tax laid by order or under the authority of the state, whether for state, county, township, or any other purpose, for the term of three years from and after the date of the patents respectively.

Little Rock Welcomes Statehood

The Hon. A. H. Sevier, our delegate in Congress, arrived last evening, direct from Washington. His entrance into our little city was quite apropos. He found our whole population in their holyday colors, just commencing a brilliant illumination of the town, and amidst the festivities and public rejoicings for our admission into the Union—an event in which he bore the leading part as one of benefactors of the state.

———

The anniversary of American independence was celebrated yesterday by a ball at the hotel of Mr. Jeffries, which, together with the illumination, gave a gay air to our town in the evening.

In the morning the Declaration of Independence was read by Mr. Clendenin, and an oration was delivered by John Field Esq., which was very creditable to him.

———

The illumination should commence at every house simultaneously. The hour of commencement, which will be announced by the ringing of the tavern bells, will be at half past eight o'clock, and it will continue one hour. It is hoped that the illumination will, as far as possible, be general. Notice issues by the Committee of Arrangements, A. Pike, T. Thorn, R. Johnson, R. H. Cocke, and L. H. Veazie.

No Rebellion by Arkansas

"The position we had assumed in regard to our state government was not correctly understood at this place (Washington)," said Delegate Ambrose H. Sevier in a letter to the *Advocate* under the date of January 1, 1836. "The impression had extended widely that Arkansas intended to form a state government and kick into nonentity the territorial authorities without the approbation of Congress.

"I have informed the president, and such others as I had an opportunity to address, that we contemplated no such thing; that rebellion or treason against the federal government never entered into the mind of a single individual in Arkansas. That we intended to form a constitution, present it to Congress for its approbation, and until it should be accepted by Congress that we expected to remain as we are in allegiance and obedience to territorial authorities. This seems satisfactory to everybody.

"Send us a republican constitution as soon as possible. Let it be here by the middle of February, and Arkansas and Michigan will be received together into the Union without difficulty."

Chapter 10

Happenings Since Statehood

The following sections are a brief synopsis of what happened in Arkansas after statehood was achieved.

From Statehood

Arkansas was admitted to the United States in 1836 as a slave state under the conditions of the Missouri Compromise. With the available river networking system, the population in Arkansas grew. River transportation allowed for trading to exist up and down the Mississippi Valley, which helped make some Arkansans moderately wealthy. The average Arkansan was able to own hogs and other livestock. The river system provided rich soil that made cotton and other farming products, such as corn and wheat, major commodities. The sharecropping system was established and helped keep the poor fed.

Arkansans, during the time of early statehood, were not all farmers and livestock breeders. The introduction of the steamboat fostered economic growth as businesses started importing home goods, manufactured goods, and clothing not available at the local stores. The numerous rivers and streams in Arkansas stimulated small water-powered factories, sawmills, and tanneries. Local craftsmen with the talent and equipment to make furniture, jewelry, and knives used the steamboats to trade up and down the Mississippi.

One famous local artisan was James Black. Mr. Black created the knife that became popularly known as the "bowie" knife. During the Antebellum Period, Arkansas could be a lawless and violent place. Men carried bowie knives, sometimes called Arkansas toothpicks, on their belts while conducting their daily business. Examples of Mr. Black's work can be seen at the Arkansas Historic Museum in Little Rock.

In the decades after statehood, the men who governed Arkansas were elected based on their personalities rather than their qualities. The voters, who had to be white males, usually elected the candidate that claimed he could secure wealth for the famers, businessmen, and crafters. The voters supported Democratic candidates and Democratic values. So very little progress was made in the interior sections of the state and there was limited interest in creating public education. The politicians supported slavery. By 1840, the Arkansas census noted that slaves made up about 20 percent of the total population. Slaves in Arkansas were treated much as they were elsewhere. Some were severely punished and mistreated. Other slaves were taught to do the work of their owners and eventually earned their freedom.

The Civil War (1861–1865)

When President Abraham Lincoln ordered the troops to respond to the Confederate attack on Fort Sumter in South Carolina, Arkansas had to make a choice. The choice was to join the Southern Confederates or remain associated with the Union. On May 6, 1861, Arkansas chose to secede from the Union and stand with the Confederacy. Arkansas was the site of over seven hundred skirmishes and battles between August of 1861 and surrender in 1865. One of the most brilliant Confederate commanders of the war was Major General Patrick Cleburne, who was referred to as the Stonewall of the West.

During the Reconstruction Period, the prices of Arkansas agricultural products dropped to a point that farmers could no longer financially prosper. Cotton, which had become the state's primary cash crop, was sold to manufacturers to be made into finished goods. Since farmers could no longer afford to produce cotton, the manufacturing businesses were devastated. To make matters worse, Arkansas's farmers were plagued by the flood of 1927. It was known as the Great Mississippi Flood. It was the worst flood the United States had ever endured. Crops up and down the Mississippi Delta were ruined as water rose and washed crops downstream. The economic impact of the flood was felt for several years afterward as prices for seed and equipment continued to climb. The farmers confronted with the increasing prices of seed and equipment and the prices of crops remaining constant fell into deeper economic distress. In 1930, the situation became worse with the Great Drought. Crops baked in the hot sun, prices of farmland dropped, and harvests were almost nonexistent. Farmers, unable to pay the bank loans required to buy seed and equipment, lost their farms and their livelihoods. Some were able to continue farming by becoming a sharecropper. Others were forced to leave the state to seek jobs in the manufacturing plants of the North. The entire nation suffered the financial collapse of Wall Street that led to a decade of economic depression.

The merchants that prospered in the early days of statehood refused to extend credit to the farmers and sharecroppers who were now destitute. No credit meant no food; farmers and their families faced starvation. When news of food riots, which were mostly peaceful and harmless, became nationally recognized, the Red Cross responded, feeding over 160,000 people.

The Impact of World War I

During the war, the agriculture demands of cotton increased with the need for uniforms and bandages to support the war effort. This resulted in an increase in the price of cotton for Arkansas farmers. The industries supporting the mining of lead and zinc saw a regrowth. Factories were open to produce the product needed, such as in Helena, Arkansas, where gunstocks were produced from local timber. Arkansas supported the training of soldiers by the construction of training facilities such as Camp Pike, now known as Camp Robinson. The camp could house thousands of soldiers from all over the United States at any one time.

The war marked a change in social, political, and economic strength from the global influence of the European world to other nations. The United States was seen as a great world power with enormous industrial strength. It was a time in history that African Americans migrated from the South to the North to obtain financial growth in northern factories.

World War II

As World War II raged in Europe, families in Arkansas again worried as their sons signed up for various branches of the armed forces and endured a multitude of changes happening at home. Everything revolved around the war effort. The needs of the servicemen came first as Arkansans lived without gasoline, car tires, and silk for hose. Rationing of food made families pool their resources to create new recipes. In addition, everyone in town and country planted small gardens called Victory Gardens to supplement their diets with nutritious fresh vegetables. Arkansans responded to campaigns to purchase war bonds to finance the war, which they believed was their civic duty. Cities like Walnut Ridge and Stuttgart received military US Army airfields.

Internment camps existed in Arkansas during World War II. The internment camps housed Japanese American citizens from California, Oregon, and Washington, just to name a few states. When the Japanese bombed Pearl Harbor on December 7, 1941, everyone of Asian descent became a terror suspect in the United States. Many of the young men signed up to join the armed forces to prove their loyalty to the US government. There were two internment camps in Arkansas: one at Rohwer and the other at Jerome. The local Arkansans did not like having foreign neighbors who were suspected terrorists, but from 1942 to 1945 over fifteen thousand Japanese Americans lived and worked at the camps. Arkansas was also elected to house German and Italian prisoners of war. The US government chose areas that were rural to keep the prisoners isolated and American families safe. Today there is almost nothing left of the once expansive camps.

After the war in Europe was won, Arkansas was back to prewar financial conditions. The state government had not developed the roads or schools that citizens needed. Arkansas's status as a rural state had been necessary to the government during the war. After the war the government closed the camps, the airfields were no longer used, and men returned home with a new worldview. During the postwar years until 1950, thousands of young couples left the state to move north to the manufacturing plants in Michigan, leaving the rural life of Arkansas behind them.

For the young men that chose to stay in their home state, the war on corruption became their new front. Since the days when Arkansas was just a territory, corruption in politics had been the norm. In fact, the men who governed Arkansas were referred to as "the Family" because they were related to one another by blood, marriage, or contract. Young veterans like Sidney McMath became involved in the reform movement. McMath campaigned for prosecuting attorney and won. He arrested a notorious political boss, Leo McLaughlin, and put him on trial. A political boss uses his power to make sure he always wins, and McMath was not able to win the court case against him. However, Mr. McMath's reputation for being a good politician won him the governor's position. As governor, McMath worked to make Arkansas more industrialized, like Michigan, and helped working-class citizens by raising the minimum wage. He also appointed the first African Americans to state organizations and increased state funding of Arkansas Agricultural, Mechanical, and Normal College, which is now known as the University of Arkansas at Pine Bluff. Additionally, in 1948, Silas Hunt became the first African American to enroll at the University of Arkansas School of Law. A few months later, Edith Irby became the first African American woman to enroll at the School of Medicine of the University of Arkansas. Change was coming to Arkansas, and the old times of impoverished rural farmers and barefoot children were thankfully ending.

In 1954, the landmark Supreme Court case *Brown v. the Board of Education* dictated that schools in the South be desegregated "with all deliberate speed." In Lawrence County, the small city of Hoxie was the first to fully integrate their schools in the fall of 1955. Although the school board faced opposition from outside forces, they refused to give in, seating African American and white students side by side in every classroom.

Desegregation of schools in the capitol city was not as easy. Many political leaders were angry with Governor Orville Faubus because he quietly allowed integration in Hoxie. In 1956, Faubus had to promise to protect segregated schools to win reelection as governor. He and his administration were not prepared for the difficulties that fulfilling that promise would cause.

Governor Faubus faced a difficult choice in the fall of 1957. First the US Supreme Court and federal law required him to allow African American students to enroll and attend Central High School. On the other hand, Governor Faubus had promised to keep schools segregated to win the election in 1956. To hold onto his political power in Arkansas, Faubus defied the federal law and used the Arkansas branch of the National Guard to stop nine African American students from going to school at Central High. The president of the United States, Dwight Eisenhower, called Faubus and personally negotiated the desegregation of Central High School.

On September 23, 1957, the nine students, supported by civil rights activist Daisy Bates, reentered Central High School. President Eisenhower sent the 101st Airborne to protect the students and enforce the law. Television cameras captured the moment as nine African American students made history. Throughout the year, the US troops or National Guard members walked students to class, kept watch in the halls, and protected them from the violence of segregation supporters. Later, in May 1958, Earnest Green became the first African American to graduate from Central High School. The desegregation of Arkansas schools helped to promote continued political reform and interracial cooperation.

Chapter 11

Arkansas Annals 1836–1936

1836

President Andrew Jackson signed the Act of Congress which admitted Arkansas to the Union. Lots were sold at public auction in the town of Ozark, county seat of Franklin. The general assembly, as authorized by the Constitution, met in joint session and elected a supreme court. However, despite the rude surroundings and the democratic simplicity of its beginnings, that first setting of the court was not wanting in dignity.

1837

The treasurer of Arkansas received from the secretary of the treasury of the United States drafts for $95,000. Major Richard B. Lee of Virginia, of the Less of Virginia, began construction of the Little Rock Arsenal in May 1837. In June the governor called an election to find a successor for Archibald Yell because his term was expired. M. Lewis Randolph, former secretary of the territory of Arkansas and grandson of Thomas Jefferson, died in Clark County. On November 6, the first special session of the state legislature was convened. Ambrose Sevier was reelected without an opponent to the Senate. Archibald Yell, a Jacksonian Democrat, was elected to the House of Representatives for Congress. The Bar Association of the state of Arkansas was established in Little Rock.

1838

The first steamboat ferry arrived in Little Rock. Reverend Leonidas Polk was elected as the missionary bishop of the Episcopal Church in Arkansas. At the second general election in Arkansas, the candidates were described as either Whigs or Democrats. The statehouse of representatives was made up of seventeen Whigs and thirty-two

Democrats; the Senate was made up of thirteen Democrats and four Whigs. The Grand Masonic Lodge of Arkansas was established. Land was purchased for the establishment of a state penitentiary.

1839

The second General Assembly granted charters for two different railroad companies to run lines in Arkansas. The first commercial bakery was established in Little Rock, "City Bakery." The town of Pine Bluff had its first theatrical performance. The first "firefighting engine" was brought to Little Rock.

1840

Little Rock suffered its first major disaster by way of a fire in the business districts of the town. Monticello was established. A public merchant house and public bath were opened in Little Rock. Little Rock suffered the worst tornado so far in Arkansas history. Lots for the town of Conway were sold to the public. Archibald Yell was elected governor of Arkansas. William Henry Harrison was elected president of the United States of America.

1841

The Arsenal at Little Rock was completed. The steamboat Odessa dropped off 170 passengers, 130 were immigrants wishing to settle in Arkansas. President William Henry Harrison passed away. The Methodist Society of Arkansas established a temperance meeting in Pope County, the first of its kind.

1842

The census records are released that say the Little Rock currently has 1,531 people, including women and slaves. The town of Arkadelphia was chosen as the county seat of Clark County. The governor approved lands to be taken from Union County and made into the new county of Ouachita. Governor Yell also approved for the formation of Montgomery County, with lands to be taken from Hot Springs County. The towns of Fort Smith and Van Buren were incorporated into Arkansas. The formations of Newton County—taking lands from Carroll County, Fulton County, and Izard County—were also approved.

1843

An act of the general assembly provided for the liquidation of the Real Estate Bank of Arkansas. The General Assembly also approved an act that made it unlawful for any person to be imprisoned for any debt unless the defendant was also found guilty of fraud. The state bank was put in the process of liquidation as a result of $1,519,623 of capital being lost. The first library in Arkansas was founded by William H. Woodruff. The *Arkansas Banner* newspaper was founded.

1844

Madame d'Estimauville opened a finishing school for the instruction of girls in Little Rock. The Rev. Andrew Byrne was consecrated as the first bishop of the Diocese of Arkansas. Governor Archibald Yell resigned to make time for his nomination to Congress. Thomas S. Drew was elected governor of the state of Arkansas. General Zachary Taylor and his family made a trip to Little Rock. The Arkansas Railroad and Transportation Company were incorporated by the general assembly.

1845

The county of Dallas was formed out of territory from Bradley and Clark Counties. July 8 was observed as a memorial service in Little Rock for General Jackson. The auditor of the state of Arkansas allowed for the purchase of $1,515.84 worth of school books to be distributed throughout the counties in Arkansas. The governor approved amendments to the Arkansas Constitution, including "no bank or banking institution shall be incorporated or established in the state."

1846

News of war with Mexico reached the state, and Governor Drew issued a preliminary proclamation urging men to volunteer. A census was ordered for the state of Arkansas. The results were 59,306 white males, 39,176 white females, 589 free blacks, and 32,261 slaves, for a total of 141,332 people in the state of Arkansas. There are forty-eight counties in Arkansas. William H. Woodruff, founder of the *Arkansas Gazette*, founded a new newspaper named the *Arkansas Democrat*. This newspaper caters to the following of the Democratic Party. Forces were raised throughout the state in aiding in the war with Mexico. Prairie and Drew Counties were established in Arkansas.

1847

The Little Rock Fire Company, which was still a volunteer firefighting company, elected William H. Woodruff as president. The Arkansas Cavalry in Mexico suffered. Yell's regiment of mounted volunteers participated in the Battle of Buena Vista, where he was charged and killed by a lance. On March 5, news reached Arkansas of the capture of fifty-three men from Arkansas by the Mexicans, including Captain Albert Pike. The first iron foundry in Arkansas was established in Little Rock. J. S. Roane and Albert Pike partook in a duel within the Cherokee Nation. Two shots were fired, both missed each man, and therefore friends of the two decided to end the conflict since honor had been suited both men.

1848

Ambrose H. Sevier, a US senator, resigned from his office so that he could go on a peacemaking mission to Mexico. Governor Thomas S. Drew appointed Major Solon Borland to the US Senate to replace Ambrose H. Sevier. Senator Chester Ashley passed away and was replaced by William K. Sebastian of Phillips County. The first high school in Arkansas was established in Little Rock, with the election of Albert Pike as president of the school board. The first bookstore was founded in Arkansas by Lemuel R. Lincoln. Ashley County was formed. Governor Drew resigned, and John Selden Roane was elected as his temporary replacement.

1849

The Clarksville Institute was incorporated as the "State Blind Asylum." Immigrants from New York passed through Little Rock on their way to California because of the great gold rush. The Little Rock Association of Steamboat Pilots was established. The Southwestern and Arkansas Mining Company was established. J. S. Roane was elected as governor of Arkansas. Fort Smith saw more and more immigrants passing through on their way to California. The Great Western US Mail Line was announced as ready to begin operations on a regular schedule.

1850

The 1850 census was released, and the city of Little Rock had a population of 2,006, of which 460 were slaves. The state penitentiary at Little Rock was burned down at about two o'clock in the morning. Pea Ridge was established as a post office. The first kindergarten was established at Little Rock. The first monthly magazine was established in Arkansas, the *Tulip*. Arkansas Military Institute was established as the former Alexander Military Institute. The state census of Arkansas shows 198,796 in total population in the state. Bishop Byrne returned from Ireland, where he went to recruit immigrants to Arkansas as a result of the recent agricultural disasters. The Masons and Odd Fellows of Little Rock made the joint decision to erect a meeting lodge in Little Rock.

1851

The town of Napoleon was incorporated into the state of Arkansas. The town of St. Charles was laid out. The theater in Arkansas was opened in Little Rock. Congress passed an act dividing Arkansas into two judicial districts. The general assembly passed an act establishing a district school in every township in Arkansas. Delegates from the different Masonic chapters in Arkansas assembled and organized the Grand Royal Arch Chapter of the state of Arkansas. The citizens of Little Rock donated a block of granite to the Washington Monument. The Arkansas Grand Lodge of Masons announced the location of the future St. John's College a few miles outside of Little Rock.

1852

The Arkansas Central Railroad Company was incorporated. Donations were asked for in regard to the formation of a public school house in Little Rock. Howe's sewing machine was introduced to the state of Arkansas. The *Christian Teacher* was released as the first purely Christian paper in Arkansas. Elias N. Conway was elected governor of Arkansas. Governor Conway established Columbia County, the fifty-fourth county in Arkansas.

1853

The general assembly passed an act dividing Arkansas into two congressional districts. St. Andrews Academy, the first Catholic school in Little Rock, opened for its second session. The People's Insurance Company of Osceola was incorporated into the state as the first fire insurance company. A fire broke out in Little Rock, destroying about twelve business buildings. The US Congress passed the Cairo and Fulton Railroad land bill. Former Arkansas Governor Drew was appointed superintendent of Indian Affairs of the Southern Superintendence. The Marine Hospital at Napoleon was completed.

1854

The most destructive fire yet to hit Little Rock destroyed much of the better buildings in the business district. Dr. Matthew Cunningham, the first resident of Little Rock, died. William R. Miller of Batesville took over the duties as auditor of the state. The state legislature had yet to reach an agreement regarding the length of the new railroad to be built—that is whether it would begin at Memphis or Cairo.

1855

Governor Conway told the general assembly they must reach an agreement on the start of the railroad quickly; they decided upon a site opposite Memphis in Hopefield. The Little Rock and Fort Smith Railroad companies were incorporated by an act of the legislature. Governor Conway elected special accountants to look into the issue of the bank. The *Arkansas Sentinel* was founded at Napoleon. The Know Nothing Party members of Arkansas had a meeting in Little Rock. The *Chronicle* was founded as a Know Nothing constituent.

1856

The Know Nothing Party, which had a great following in late 1855, was on the decline because of its leanings toward the abolitionist movement. Both the Democrats and the Know Nothings had party meetings in Arkansas and elected their respective delegates. Elias Conway was reelected governor of Arkansas. The governor released a statement about the occupants of the state penitentiary, including ninety inmates.

1857

Governor Conway signed an act that abolished the Swamp Lands Commission. Dr. David Dale Owen was assigned as state geologist. The agricultural societies of White and Prairie Counties had the first fairgrounds at Des Arc to exhibit various agricultural products. Governor Conway elected James S. Williams as chief engineer on the Cairo and Fulton Railroad.

1858

Springfield, seat of Conway County, was hit by a devastating tornado. The First and Second Congressional District Democratic Conventions were held in Batesville and Camden, respectively. A pamphlet was widespread throughout the state urging Arkansans to remove all their "Negroes from the state." The first Little Rock high school for girls opened. The town clock of Little Rock was installed. Dr. David Dale Owen released *Geological Reconnaissance of Arkansas*.

1859

The *Arkansas Baptist* was founded at Little Rock, the first Baptist newspaper of its kind in Arkansas. The first coeducational high school was opened in Pine Bluff, called Jefferson High School. The Arkansas Institute for the Blind was incorporated into the state. Governor

Conway signed a legislative act for the removal of "all free Negroes and mulattoes" over twenty-one years of age by January 1860. The Arkansas Baptist State Convention was established. Arkansas College at Fayetteville conferred the first ever master of arts degree in the state. The Pulaski County Agricultural and Mechanical Society was founded.

1860

Henry M. Rector defeated Richard H. Johnson for the position of governor of Arkansas. St. Mary's Academy held its first commencement in Little Rock. The first telegraph line in Arkansas went into operation between St. Louis, Missouri, and Fayetteville, Arkansas. Arkansas, in the presidential election of 1860, choose John C. Breckenridge with 28,732 votes, Abraham Lincoln received zero votes from the state of Arkansas. The first Arkansas state fair was held at Little Rock. The telegraph lines from Little Rock to Pine Bluff and from Memphis to Des Arc were completed.

1861

The census for the state of Arkansas was released with a white population of 325,000 and a slave population of 110,450. On January 15, Governor Rector signed for an election deciding whether Arkansas should secede from the Union. The Little Rock Arsenal surrendered to the state. The Secession Convention was put together to decide whether Arkansas should secede or stay as part of the Union, while other parts of the state vowed their support and allegiance to the Confederacy. On May 6, Arkansas seceded from the Union. On May 10, Arkansas passed an ordinance accepting the Constitution of the Confederate States of America. On May 13 the Secession Convention created a military board. On May 30 the First Arkansas Confederate Calvary was raised. On November 9 Arkansas meets to elect senators for the Confederate States of America.

1862

The Memphis and Little Rock Railroad was completed. St. John's College was chosen to serve as a temporary hospital for the wounded. The first battle of the Civil War to be fought on Arkansas soil was at Elkhorn Tavern, Pea Ridge. The battle made apparent the need for more hospitals in the state. Many Arkansans fought in the battle of Shiloh and suffered great loss. Governor Rector issued another immediate proclamation calling for volunteers. Harris Flanagin was elected governor of Arkansas.

1863

The Union Army at Helena was put under the command of General Ulysses S. Grant. Brigadier General Thomas J. Churchill surrendered the fortified position at Arkansas Post to Union forces. Acts of vandalism were reported throughout the state as a result of the Union forces. The siege of Vicksburg was ended by the surrender of the Confederates, which ultimately cut Arkansas off from the rest of the war. In fear for the safety of Little Rock, the state government moved the seat of government to Washington, Hempstead County. The *Arkansas Democrat-Gazette* were put under Union control under orders from General Frederick Steele.

1864

David O. Dodd was publicly hanged in front of St. John's College at age seventeen for allegations of being a Confederate spy. The infantry of the army of Arkansas were ordered from Camden to Louisiana to aid General Taylor in the Red River Campaign. Arkansas's Confederate forces were defeated at the Battle of Jenkins's Ferry.

1865

Arkansas Confederate troops were encamped at Washington, Arkansas, for the winter. Governor Flanagin called for Arkansas planters to send cotton to San Antonio in exchange for medicine and supplies. General E. Kirby, upon knowing of General Lee's surrender, surrendered the

Arkansas troops at Baton Rouge, Louisiana. A People's Convention met at Little Rock to discuss the newly formed Union government.

1866

Authorization was made for the First National Bank of Fort Smith. An Arkansas Confederate Memorial Association was organized in Little Rock. Arkansas elected John T. Jones and Andrew Hunter as the new senators to the United States of America. The two joined with other members of the general assembly in a trip to Washington to discuss the state of political union. A legislative committee reported the financial distress on behalf of banks, real estate, and state.

1867

The Arkansas Institute for the Blind reopened. Daily mail began to run regularly again throughout Arkansas. The commissioners the state elected to go to Washington to confer about political distress came home with a full report. Andrew Hunter refused to be a US senator, and therefore a general assembly was convened to fill the vacancy. A Union State Convention met at the capitol. St. John's College was reopened. The German Immigrant Aide Society was formed in Little Rock. General E. O. C. Ord, commander of the Fourth Military District, issued from his headquarters at Vicksburg a decree of the rightful delegates to Arkansas's Constitutional Convention—of those, eight were African Americans.

1868

A new state constitution was adopted with the aid of the Special Act of Congress; twenty-two delegates refused to sign the new constitution. The legislature, by joint resolution, ratified the Fourteenth Amendment. Powell Clayton was inaugurated as governor of Arkansas. The "invisible empire" of the Ku Klux Klan was forming in Arkansas. Governor Clayton was involved in a military scandal known as the Hesper Affair. In Arkansas, Ulysses S. Grant was chosen president.

1869

A number of counties were relieved from martial law. Governor Clayton called for the establishment of Grant County. Governor Clayton approved an act to fund the debt of the state of Arkansas. The county of Boone was created in honor of Daniel Boone. Officers of the Masonic Grand Lodge of Arkansas laid the cornerstone for the College of Dover. The Arkansas Deaf Mute Institute and Arkansas School for the Blind were laid in motion. The first African American newspaper began in Arkansas, called the *Arkansas Freeman*. The Arkansas Teachers' Association was organized at Little Rock.

1870

The Western Union Telegraph Company ran a line from Little Rock to Arkadelphia. The city council ordered Little Rock to number the houses and rename the streets in the city. The Cairo and Fulton Railroad was now a work in progress. The first street car company was incorporated in Arkansas. Congress passed a bill for $100,000 to erect a government building at Little Rock.

1871

Clayton left the office of governor to pursue the office of senate, of which he was elected. Clayton still had his factions controlling the state government but felt he was threatened; he therefore did not become senator. He did eventually accept the office of senator, and the office of governor was filled by Ozra A. Hadley, a close friend of Clayton. Governor Hadley signed into effect Nevada, Sarber, and Lincoln Counties. Arkansas Industrial University was announced as the first state university.

1872—January 22

The Arkansas Industrial University opened its doors for the receipt of students, with N. P. Gates as president. The university was then without buildings, except for one six-room dwelling. The citizens of Fayetteville and Washington Counties remodeled this dwelling and erected a two-story frame structure for the temporary use of school. Fayetteville had been selected as the site for the university on September 18, 1871, by a board of trustees elected at a joint session of the legislature on March 25, 1871.

1873—January 4
A state convention of political supporters of Joseph Brooks was held at Little Rock to protest against the seating of Elisha Baxter as governor. On the same day, Governor Hadley, "for the safety of state property," ordered Mayor General D. P. Uphan to post a sufficient force of state troops to protest and preserve the capital building of this state. It was generally understood that this action on the part of Governor Hadley was taken because of the apprehension that certain members of the general assembly might join in a move to install Brooks as governor and set up a rival state government.

1874
The Brooks–Baxter War began. After court action, Brooks took possession of the governor's office. Armed men gathered on Markham Street. President Grant recognized Baxter as governor.

1874—April 18
Steamboat *Mary Boyd* arrived at Little Rock early in the morning from Pine Bluff, loaded with three hundred armed men for the reinforcement of Baxter forces. The recruits, commanded by Ira McBarton and H. K. White, were mostly Negroes. With a brass band at their head, they marched from the steamboat landing to the Anthony House, the Baxter headquarters. Brooks recognizes Baxter as governor on May 16, 1874.

1875—December 22
Miller County was reestablished by an act of the legislature out of territory taken from Lafayette County. The county was named in honor of James Miller, the first governor of the Arkansas Territory. (The first Miller County had been created by an act of the territorial legislature

of April 1, 1820, but as then organized, the county embraced territory which later was "ceded" to Texas, when the boundary between Texas and Arkansas was finally determined by an agreement between the United States and the Republic of Texas on June 24, 1841.)

1876—September 4

Arkansas held its first biennial election under the constitution of 1874, which provided that the governor and other constitutional officers of the state should be elected biennially "on the first Monday of September," unless the general assembly should see fit to fix a different date. The entire Democratic ticket was elected. For governor, William R. Miller received 70,425 votes; A. W. Bishop, Republican, received 38,208. Of those elected to the general assembly all but eighteen were Democrats. Most of the Republicans were members of the House; there were five Negro Republicans in the House.

1877—January 16

Augustus H. Garland, at a joint session of the general assembly, was elected US senator, to succeed Powell Clayton. Garland's term was to begin March 4. T. D. W. Yonley was the only other candidate. Garland received 113 votes on the first ballot, Yonley received 8. Of the 18 Republicans in the legislature, ten voted for Garland, five of which were Negroes.

1878—July 20

The Greenback Party held its state convention at Little Rock. It had been the intention of the leaders to nominate Henry M. Rector (governor of Arkansas, 1860–1862) for governor, but he declared his allegiance to the Democratic Party, in spite of his endorsements of the Greenback principles. The convention adjourned without nominating a candidate. (Because of the friendly attitude of the Negro leaders toward the administration of Governor Miller, the Republican Party refrained from nominating candidates for state offices.)

1879—March 10

The Western Union Telegraph Company installed at Little Rock the first telephones used in Arkansas. The Little Rock "Exchange," which was put into service a few months later with no subscribers, is said to have been the third exchange established in the United States.

1880—September 6

In the biennial state election, Thomas Churchill, the Democratic candidate for governor, received 84,088 votes. W. P. Parks, the Greenback candidate, received 31,284. The other Democratic candidates for state office were elected by similar majorities.

1881—March 9

Governor Churchill signed an act of the legislature, regulating the practice of medicine and surgery and creating a state board of health. The governor also signed the first act prohibiting the carrying of concealed weapons.

1882—January 14

Governor T. J. Churchill, General Grandison Royston, and Professor Lee Thompson inspected the Branch Normal College for Negroes at Pine Bluff as required by the legislature. The building had been completed at a cost of $9,600. T. Hardin was architect and the contractors were Hardin and Bailey of Little Rock. Professor Corbin was in charge of the school. The Arkansas State Bar Association was organized at Little Rock at a meeting of members of the bar from all sections of Arkansas.

1883—January 8

The twenty-fourth general assembly convened. J. B. Judkins was elected president of the Senate, and W. C. Braley was elected Speaker of the House.

1884—October 21

The Democratic State Convention met in Little Rock to nominate a candidate for chief justice of Arkansas. On the fifty-ninth ballot, Sterling Lockrill was nominated.

1885—October 15

Connection was made from Little Rock to Pine Bluff by the Arkansas Telegraph Company. At Pine Bluff the line connected with the Baltimore and Ohio Telegraph Company.

1886—November 11

The first passenger train over the Batesville and Brinkley railroad arrived at Jacksonport.

1887—January 24

The Army and Navy Hospital at Hot Springs opened.

1888—May 1

The first state convention of the Union Labor Party nominated C. M. Norwood as a candidate for governor, and it named other candidates and delegates to the national convention.

1889—April 4

The general assembly passed acts including increasing the membership of the Supreme Court to five; placing the compensation of members of the general assembly at six dollars per day, and their traveling allowance at ten cents a mile; and giving county courts the right to levy road improvement taxes and the power to fix the boundary lines of levee districts.

1890—February 16

The assessed value of Arkansas property for 1889 was $172,241,726. Personal property was $62,171,391.

1891—January 7
Dr. John C. Branner, chief of the geological survey, reported to Governor Eagle that he had discovered a bauxite deposit in Saline County that he considered one of the greatest in the United States.

1892—September 6
Colonel W. M. Fishback and the entire Democratic ticket were elected in the state general election. Amendment No. 2, the Poll Tax Amendment, carried.

1893
On February 16 Governor Fishback issued a proclamation announcing the adoption of Amendment No. 2, known as the Poll Tax Amendment. On April 12 Sterling Cockrill tendered his resignation as Chief Justice of the Arkansas Supreme Court to Governor Fishback. Judge James W. Butler of Batesville, judge of the third judicial circuit, was appointed to fill the vacancy.

1894—February 12
A bill authorizing the construction of a bridge over the Arkansas River at Van Buren by the Fort Smith and Van Buren Railway was passed by the House of Representatives.

1895—April 25
Alexander Graham Bell, inventor of the telephone, spent the day in Little Rock.

1896—September 8
The contract for the construction of the free bridge across the Arkansas River at the foot of main channel was awarded to the Grafton Bridge Company of New York.

1897—January 4
The thirty-first general assembly convened. Jeff Davis of Pope County was elected messenger to take the Arkansas presidential veto to Washington.

1898—April 22

The president called for 1,600 troops from Arkansas to serve in the war against Spain.

1898—July 14

Three companies of Arkansas Negro troops left for the Jefferson Barracks to train for service in the Spanish-American War.

1899—April 15

Senator J. D. Kimbell's bill providing for the construction of a million-dollar state capitol on the penitentiary grounds was passed by the House.

1899—November 16

The plans for the new state capitol prepared by George R. Mann were adopted by the State Capitol Commission.

Chapter 12

<u>Chronological Review 1900–1950</u>

In the following review of events which made news in Arkansas in the period beginning in 1900, news stories were selected at random from musty and yellowed files. Items which affected large sections of the state or Arkansas as a whole were selected on the basis of interest and significance. The reader may use this review in recalling these same historical incidents, each of which may be considered a stepping-stone in the history of Arkansas.

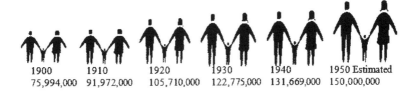

1900	1910	1920	1930	1940	1950 Estimated
75,994,000	91,972,000	105,710,000	122,775,000	131,669,000	150,000,000

US Population Doubles in Fifty Years: These figures above show how the population of the United States has grown since the turn of the century. In 1900, the country was made up of 75,994,000 citizens. The estimated number of US residents in 1950 was 150,000,000. A census is under way now to determine the official number.

Significant Dates

1900

Jeff Davis, Democratic nominee for Congress, won the election, defeating H. L. Remmel, a Republican, and A. W. Files, a Populist. Also that year, William J. Bryan, Democratic candidate for president, received 81,142 votes in Arkansas. His opponent, William McKinley, received 44,800 votes in Arkansas.

A freight car containing hundreds of bushels of Irish potatoes, sweet potatoes, and onions was sent from Little Rock to the Galveston flood sufferers.

The first train over the Little Rock and Hot Springs Railroad arrived in Little Rock from the resort city. W. H. "Coin" Harvey of Monte Ne addressed a large audience at Eureka Springs on the "free silver" question.

1901

Joe T. Robinson, a Lonoke attorney, announced that he would be a candidate for Congress from the sixth district.

A temperature of 106 degrees was recorded in Little Rock on

July 12, the highest temperature recorded up to that date by the US Weather Bureau since the office was opened on July 1, 1879.

Labor Day was celebrated in Little Rock by a parade and speeches at West End Park by Governor Jeff Davis; T. H. Humphreys, speaker of the House of Representatives; Senator Creed Caldwell; and H. L. Remmel.

1902

A disastrous sleet storm causing $500,000 in damage struck Little Rock. Most business houses sustained some damage, and tree limbs and telephone and telegraph wires were pulled down.

Scott Street Methodist Church, on Fourteenth and Scott Streets, was dedicated. Eleven students graduated from the University of Arkansas Medical Department. The Choctaw, Oklahoma, and Gulf Railroad was purchased by the Rock Island Co.

The Scottish Rite Consistory, on Eighth and Scott Streets, was formally dedicated, with a number of Masonic dignitaries present for the occasion.

Madison County courthouse at Huntsville burned, along with a hotel and several business houses and residences. Loss was placed at fifty thousand dollars.

1903

The cornerstone of the new YMCA building, on Capitol and Scott Streets, was laid with impressive ceremony. A number of YMCA, church, and civic leaders were present for the occasion. George T. Coxhead of St. Louis, who organized the Little Rock YMCA in 1883, made one of the principal addresses.

It was on the site of the new building at Capitol and Scott Streets that Chester Ashley and Amos Wheeler, early citizens, built a two-room house for the occupancy of the Arkansas Territorial Legislature. The legislature met there from 1821 to 1835.

George W. Donaghey of Conway was elected superintendent of the work of constructing the foundation for the new state capitol. Contract for the building was let for $947,000.

Voters of Argenta (North Little Rock) cast their ballots—475 to 44—in favor of separation from Little Rock.

1904

Arkansas took part in the World's Fair at St. Louis by setting up a building and exhibit costing $17,500. Twelve State Guard companies and numerous delegations of state citizens went to St. Louis to take part in proceedings and to visit the fair. Arkansas won first prize for its display of fresh fruits at the fair.

A tragic fire destroyed twenty-two business firms, six homes, the Masonic Temple, and the post office at Lake Village. A fire in the Prescott business and residential district entailed a loss of $75,000. Rector suffered a fire in a block of buildings in that city and the loss was placed at $75,500.

A group of fourteen German capitalists from northern states purchased twenty thousand acres of land in Jefferson County on which to establish a colony of German farmers. E. E. Barclay, vice president of the Gould Railway System, brought the men to Arkansas.

1905

Governor Jeff Davis signed the Logan-King antitrust bill, causing many insurance companies to withdraw from the state.

The bridge across the Arkansas River at Fort Smith, a $750,000 structure, was completed. In Little Rock, the river was frozen over.

A fire in Hot Springs caused six deaths and property damage of $1,250,000. About forty blocks were destroyed in the southern part of the city.

Arkansas monuments to the Confederate dead were unveiled on the lawn of the new state capitol.

The building on E. Markham Street, occupied by the Arkansas Democrat, was destroyed by fire with a loss of $180,000 on July 24.

Travel between Arkansas and Louisiana was restricted due to a yellow fever epidemic in New Orleans. Arkansas State Guard enforced quarantines at border cities.

President Theodore Roosevelt visited Little Rock on October 25. He delivered a short address before an enthusiastic crowd, and visited Fort Roots and other points of interest.

Construction on the Hotel Marion was started.

1906

Diamonds were discovered in the neighborhood of Hickory Creek, Pike County, near Murfreesboro, by John Wesley Huddleston, on August 1. Sam W. Reyburn of Little Rock obtained an option on a 360-acre tract where the stones were found. Many other persons also invested in property in the area.

Returns from the Democratic primary showed that Jeff Davis was nominated to the United States Senate. John S. Little was nominated for governor and took office at the end of the year.

Mme. Sarah Bernhardt made an appearance at Forest Park as part of her farewell tour of America. Since difficulties prevented her from appearing at the Capital Theater, she was forced to go to the summer theater five miles west of the city.

Transportation difficulties did not keep followers of the "Divine Sarah" from seeing the performance. Standing room was at a premium and ticket "scalpers" found quick sales of their seats at five dollars each. Some even got ten dollars for a single ticket.

Mme. Bernhardt appeared in *Camille*. The *Democrat* commented, "The fact that not one in a hundred of the audience understood a word of the French dialogue did not seem to detract one iota from the intense enjoyment of the pantomimic portrayal of the well-known story of Camille and her lover, Armand Duval."

People from all parts of the state attended the show. There were at least 2,000 in the audience, and 1,900 paid admissions were reported.

Streetcar riders, at least some of them, did not arrive until after the first act since the current was too weak to operate as many cars as were needed to carry the immense throng to the theater.

A reviewer commented: "There were the usual number of gossipers, also, who careless of the demands of good breeding and the feelings of their neighbors, persisted in carrying on a hum of conversation even during the emotional moments."

A contract for construction of a car factory in Pine Bluff was let in February by the Cotton Belt Railway Co. The factory was to cost between $150,000 and $200,000.

Here is a list of significant dates in Little Rock history prior to 1900.

- March 1820: A post office was established in Little Rock, with Amos Wheeler as postmaster.
- July 4, 1820: The first sermon was preached in Little Rock by the Reverend Cephas Washburn, on his way to found the Cherokee mission.
- June 1, 1821: Little Rock was made the capital of the Territory of Arkansas.
- March 22, 1822: The steamboat *Eagle*, moving upstream, arrived at Little Rock, the first steamboat to come up the Arkansas River that far.
- 1822: The first white child was born in Little Rock, a boy to Dr. Matthew and Eliza (Wilson) Cunningham.
- 1825: The first office building was erected, made out of a row of log houses on the north side of Markham Street from Main Street to the first alley west.
- 1825: The first church was built in the city by the Baptists, on the block bounded by Main, Third, Scott, and Fourth Streets.
- 1826: A brickyard was opened by Christian Brumbagh and Benjamin Clements.
- November 7, 1831: Little Rock was incorporated as a town.
- January 8, 1835: The first common seal for the city was adopted.
- September 12, 1836: The first state legislature assembled in Little Rock. James S. Conway was governor.
- June 27, 1838: A steamboat ferry was established in Little Rock across the Arkansas River.
- 1860: Gas lights were installed on the streets.
- February 8, 1861: The arsenal in City Park (now MacArthur Park) was evacuated by United States troops and turned over to the state.
- September 10, 1863: Little Rock was occupied by Federal forces under the command of General Frederick Steele.

- 1869: The first school board was organized by the city. In that year, there was only one school building, located where Peabody School was built later.
  - 1874: The first railroad bridge (Baring Cross Bridge) was built across the Arkansas River.
  - July 1, 1879: The US Weather Bureau in Little Rock was opened for public inspection.
  - May 4, 1888: Water was turned into the mains of the city by the Little Rock waterworks. Before this, a "standpipe" system had been used.
  - December 1, 1890: The Confederate Soldiers' Home was opened at Sweet Home, southeast of the city.
  - October 2, 1894: A tornado which struck Little Rock caused an estimated one million dollars in damage. Two persons were killed and forty injured.
  - November 27, 1900: The cornerstone of the new capitol building was laid by the Arkansas Grand Lodge of Freemasonry.

Production capacity of the unit was to be forty boxcars per month, with other facilities for passengers and special cars.

Conway and Pope County farmers and businessmen formed a Horticultural Agricultural Association on January 26, 1906, in Morrilton. The purpose of the group was to promote better methods in agriculture and horticulture and to bring about diversification of crops. The Missouri Pacific-Iron Mountain horticultural agent addressed the association.

Mistakes made by surveyors threw Hot Springs property owners in turmoil in February. An error of seventy feet was made in the calculations of an area on upper Park Avenue, one of the city's thoroughfares.

Property owners, checking with the official plat of the area, found that many of their houses stood in the middle of streets and several alleys ran through parlors. Residents sought court action to have boundaries changed.

Justice was tempered with mercy by a Little Rock police court judge. The judge revealed that when drunks were brought before him, especially heads of families, he would "give them a chance." He prepared a pledge for convicted drunks to sign declaring that they would abstain from "intoxicating liquors of every kind and character" for certain periods. The length of time for the abstinence varied according to the punishment, which the judge wished to place upon the culprits. Drunks were warned that if they were found drinking the time named in the pledge that they would be arrested and required to pay a fine.

1907

Governor John S. Little suffered a breakdown in January, and Senator X. O. Pindall became acting governor to handle duties of the office.

A fire destroyed 150 dwellings in a nine-block area in Pine Bluff. Loss was $250,000.

The legislature established a two-cent fare for railroads, which declared their intentions of continuing to charge three cents per passenger mile, and prepared to contest the two-cent act in court.

Rock Island Lines announced beginning of construction of

Biddle Shops in the southeastern part of Little Rock. Properties planned were a roundhouse, terminals, yards and shops.

A fire destroyed 2,415 bales of cotton in the Gulf Compress Co., Baring Cross, North Little Rock.

Conway was chosen for the site of the State Normal School, after a contest between Benton, Russellville, Quitman, Fort Smith, and Conway.

The legislature passed a bill which would prohibit the sale of cigarettes in Arkansas. The bill did not become a law.

The *Southwest American* was established in Fort Smith.

1908

George W. Donaghey won the Democratic nomination for governor defeating Attorney General Kirby.

Construction on the Little Rock Public Library was begun.

The Carnegie Library was opened in Fort Smith the same year.

Fourteen persons were killed in a tornado which struck Hot Springs.

1909

President William Howard Taft visited in Little Rock and spoke from a platform at Union Station. This was the third time in its history that Little Rock had entertained a president of the United States.

Mrs. M. M. Cohn, wife of a leading merchant of Little Rock, was killed in a street car accident in Chicago.

A Southern Methodist Educational rally in Little Rock raised $50,800 for Hendrix College in Conway in two days.

1910

Railroads continued to expand in the state with several new ones completed in 1910. These included a twenty-two-mile line from Mesa to Stuttgart on Rock Island and a sixteen-mile line on the Fort Smith, Scranton, and Eastern that connected the Arkansas Central at Paris with the new town of Scranton in Logan County.

The nineteenth annual reunion of the Blue and Gray was held in Heber Springs, with Senator Jeff Davis as the principal speaker.

Construction of an agricultural school at Jonesboro was announced.

The cornerstone of Calhoun County's new courthouse was laid. The building to be replaced was built in 1858.

1911

The governor of New Jersey delivered a brief speech in Little Rock. His name was Woodrow Wilson.

Tornadoes in April killed three persons in Plumerville and destroyed considerable property in Mena.

About forty thousand people visited Little Rock to attend a reunion of Confederate veterans.

Fires in Little Rock that year destroyed the entire block on the east side of Main Street between Sixth and Seventh Streets, the plant of the Big Rock Stone and Construction Co., at the foot of Fort Roots, and the plant of the Arkansas Brick and Manufacturing Co.

Little Rock residents began using natural gas.

H. K. Toney was elected president of the state Senate, and Judge R. F. Milwee was elected Speaker of the House.

1912

Heavy snows and extremely cold weather were reported throughout the state, with Rogers reporting a temperature of ten below zero. April floods caused a Mississippi River bridge to collapse, inundating five hundred thousand acres in Mississippi, Crittenden, Poinsett, and Cross Counties.

Completion of the battleship Arkansas was announced.

Colonel Theodore Roosevelt made a speaking tour of Arkansas, addressing citizens at numerous points, including a crowd of six thousand in Argenta.

Arkansas supplied the nation with an unusually large peach crop, and one carload of peaches was shipped from Highland to London, England.

Eugene V. Debs, Socialist nominee for president of the United States, spoke in Little Rock.

Grant County's circuit judge figured he had better take quick action and called a special session of circuit court to try two men charged with burglary and grand larceny. Pine Bluff and Little Rock police, who had seen the men since their capture, claimed they were two of the most notorious and dangerous criminals in the country. The judge believed that the Grant County jail was not strong enough to hold the two desperadoes very long—especially since he figured their gang would try to release them. So he decided a quick trial would be the best thing.

Fireman Jim Flynn, one of the leading boxers in the 1912 era, was sports editor of the *Democrat* for one day on April 30, 1912. This wasn't his first experience with newspapers either. He earned his first money selling papers when he was a boy. When he had the $1.50, he rushed off to a sporting goods store and purchased a pair of boxing gloves.

1913

Joe T. Robinson was sworn in as governor, succeeding George W. Donaghey. The state legislature elected W. M. Kavanaugh to succeed Jeff Davis as senator, following the latter's death.

Capitol Theater on W. Markham Street was destroyed by fire. A Hot Springs fire destroyed fifty blocks of residences and businesses, with a loss estimated at $10 million.

The cornerstone of the Leo N. Levi Hospital in Hot Springs was laid.

The US Supreme Court affirmed the Arkansas General Assembly's law fixing railroad passenger rates at two cents a mile.

A new state law ordered death for criminals by electrocution instead of by hanging. The penitentiary board began the construction of three death cells, an electrician's room, and an electric chair at the penitentiary in Little Rock.

1914

Parts of the Ninth Infantry Regiment, stationed at Fort Roots, were sent to Laredo, Texas, for border duty.

Crittenden County sold $350,000 in bonds for money to build approaches to the Harahan Bridge and for roads.

A fire destroyed the main buildings of Henderson-Brown College in Arkadelphia, with a loss placed at $80,000.

1915

Floods on the Red River cut off Little Rock's natural gas supply.

In North Little Rock, a fire destroyed the Matthews Building, between Second and Third Streets on Main Street.

Arkansas apples exhibited at the San Francisco Panama-Pacific Exposition won the first gold medal to be awarded at the fair.

The first annual convention of the Arkansas Women's Suffrage Association was held in Little Rock.

A long-distance balloon race was won by William Assman, who landed his balloon at Prescott after a flight from Wichita, Kansas.

1916

Seventy-five persons lost their lives in a tornado that swept across the state. Heber Springs was worst hit, with twenty-two dead. Floods along the Arkansas and other rivers caused at least four drownings. Arkansas City was flooded, and seven hundred residents camped on top of the levee. Steamboats carried another one thousand inhabitants out of the area and up the Mississippi.

R. C. Hall, superintendent of Little Rock schools, was elected president of the Arkansas State Teachers Association.

Cotton sold for as much as thirty-five cents a pound, with a Pine Bluff firm buying nineteen bales of long-staple cotton at that price.

1917

Charles H. Brough was inaugurated as governor and the legislature enacted a "bone-dry" law. Arkansas became the sixteenth state to have a statewide prohibition law.

Arkansas was ordered to furnish 10,267 men in the nationwide plans to draft a total of 587,000 men for the army. The site for a division camp was selected near Little Rock to care for 65,000 soldiers.

Camp Pike was built by the James Stewart Co., of St. Louis and New York. The approximate cost was $3,500. Contracts were awarded to twenty-five Arkansas mills for fifteen million feet of yellow-pine lumber for Camp Pike. General Leonard Wood, of the army, inspected the camp that year. As many as 6,500 workmen were on the payrolls at one time while the camp was being built.

One thousand officers were ordered to Fort Logan H. Roots for further training. An aviation training school at Lonoke was named Eberts Field in honor of Captain Melchior M. Eberts of the Army Signal Corps.

1918

Speeches encouraging the purchase of Liberty Bonds were made in all parts of Arkansas. Notables visiting Camp Pike included Miss Margaret Wilson, daughter of the president. She gave two concerts. William J. Bryan also spoke to the soldiers.

The Thirty-Ninth Division, which included many Arkansas men, was ordered back to the United States from France. Camp Pike was designated as a demobilization center.

Governor Brough and Senator Robinson were renominated by large majorities in the Democratic primary.

Little Rock banks, on the evening of April 6, 1918, reported a flood in the sale of Liberty Bonds and leaders in the drive predicted that the city would reach $500,000 or more by night in the third bond drive. In an address at Capitol and Main Streets, William Jennings Bryan pleaded for the Liberty Loan and also for a unified nation behind other war measures. The Pulaski County quota was $3.5 million.

1919

Prohibition in Arkansas came into full effect with the signing of the Greathouse Bill that prohibited shipment of liquor into Arkansas and from one point to another in the state.

A race riot at Elaine, south of Helena, resulted in the deaths of scores of Negroes, and five hundred soldiers from Camp Pike were sent to restore order. Seventy-five persons were given death or prison sentences for participating in the affair.

Organization of the Broadway–Main Street Bridge District was announced.

1920

Thomas C. McRae was elected governor to succeed Charles H. Brough.

T. H. Caraway defeated W. F. Kirby for US senator in the Democratic primary.

Oil well drilling activities in southern Arkansas attracted considerable attention. Land soared in price, and one gasser produced sixty million cubic feet a day.

1921

Thomas C. McRae was inaugurated as governor, succeeding Charles Hillman Brough.

A Washington announcement said that a veteran's hospital would be located at Fort Roots. The War Department ordered the abandonment of Camp Pike, which had been used as a separation center following training activities at the camp.

Little Rockians inspected the new million-dollar Missouri Pacific station that replaced the building destroyed by fire in April 1902.

Commissioners of the Broadway–Main Street Bridge District accepted the bid of the Missouri Valley Bridge and Iron Co. to build two new bridges across the river at Little Rock.

1922

Hospital facilities in Little Rock were expanded, with the city council appropriating $300,000 to complete the City Hospital (now University). The Missouri Pacific Railroad Co. authorized the erection of a hospital to cost $450,000. Expenditure of $500,000 to enlarge the government hospital at Fort Roots was announced.

The University of Arkansas announced plans to establish a rice experiment station near Stuttgart.

Checks totaling $1,380,000 were mailed to members of the Arkansas Cotton Growers Cooperative Association.

The Ku Klux Klan became active in Little Rock.

Dan Cupid had his troubles in Pulaski County during the first half of June 1922. In a fifteen-day bout with Old Man Divorce, Cupid lost the decision by winning only six rounds. Nine white couples were divorced during the period while only six couples took out wedding licenses. Arkansas's Anti-Saloon League superintendent in August 1922 charged that the effects of a national poll on prohibition would be detrimental to the cause of the "drys." He thought the United States would remain dry. The poll was being taken by the *Literary*

Digest to sound the sentiment of the people on the prohibition question. The superintendent said, in his opinion, there was no prohibition question. He said ratification of the Eighteenth Amendment had completely solved the wet–dry question, and only those who wanted a drink could be interested in such a poll.

Communications with other planets failed in June 1922. Guglielmo Marconi, an Italian radio wizard, failed to pick up any message from Mars on a trip across the Atlantic on his floating laboratory, the *Arkansas Democrat* reported. Marconi told the Associated Press, "Have no sensational announcement to make."

Dale's Blue Melody Boys presented the first radio concert ever broadcast from Little Rock on July 16, 1922.

The *Arkansas Democrat* reported "radio enthusiasts within a radius of several hundred miles of this city were treated to a Sunday evening orchestral concert, the first of its kind ever broadcast" here. The concert was presented over the station of J. C.

Dice, 3820 Compton, Pulaski Heights.

The Blue Melody Boys were playing a summer engagement at the White City dance pavilion.

Little Rock would make a good location for textile and spinning mills, a widely known consulting engineer told the Board of Commerce in 1922. Favorable conditions he listed were nearness to the cotton supply, climatic and labor conditions, and the possibility of cheap power from the hydroelectric project planned on the Little Red River.

Jonesboro officers "stilled" a still in June 1922. The law enforcement officers located a whiskey still inside a shack on the banks of Cache River, west of Bono. After setting fire to the building and the still, they destroyed a large quantity of mash found on the premises.

The alleged proprietor of the still was arrested and a quantity of moonshine liquor found in his possession.

1923

Maintenance of the state highway system as one state

project was begun under the Harrelson Highway Law.

In Hot Springs, the Arlington Hotel burned, with one fireman killed and two others injured when brick walls fell. Plans for a new Arlington Hotel got underway. The estimated cost was $2.5 million.

One man was fatally burned in Smackover when a $200,000 fire destroyed more than one block of a business building.

Large numbers of oil wells were being drilled in southern Arkansas.

1924

A dramatic escape of three convicts from the death cell of the penitentiary and the ensuing chase made big headlines in newspapers.

Directors of the American Trust Co. and the Southern Trust Co., two of the area's largest financial institutions, announced a unanimous decision to merge the two firms following a meeting on August 15, 1924. The new merged institution's assets amounted to approximately $17 million.

The merger action followed the resignation of Ed Cornish as American Trust Co. president, and the sale of his stock, along with that of the Lesser-Goldman interests, representing a controlling bloc. The stock was bought by Southern President A. B. Banks and Vice President Joe H. Stanley. Mr. Cornish, although remaining as a director of the merged bank, became president of the newly formed, $8 million National Cotton Seed Products Corp., which announced plans to operate offices both in Little Rock and Memphis. The new company, formed through the merger of many Arkansas and Tennessee firms, set up main offices in the $2 million Memphis plant of the Dixie Cotton Oil Co., which was included in the merger.

The American Trust Co. was organized in 1875 as the German National Bank and was located at Markham and Main Streets. The name was later changed to the American National Bank, and the 1924 name derived through subsequent mergers.

1925

An open field east of Little Rock was approved as a site for an intermediate air depot for the army. The action gave assurance to the city that a municipal airport would be developed.

The state's first major hydroelectric project, Remmel Dam, was dedicated.

The first state park at Petit Jean Mountain was dedicated.

J. R. Grant, state supervisor of rural schools, was elected president of the Arkansas Education Association. Charles S. McCain, president of Bankers Trust Co., resigned to become vice president of National Park Bank in New York.

Chicago Milling and Lumber Co. in Blytheville burned with a loss of $450,000. A fire in business buildings in Cotton Plant destroyed $100,000 worth of property.

Plans for erection of the Rector Building, at Third and Spring Streets, were announced.

The Little Rock Boys' Club, at Eighth and Scott Streets, was formally opened.

1926

Arkansas voters adopted an amendment authorizing a maximum school tax of $18 million, thus raising the tax from $12 million.

Mary Lewis, opera star and native of Arkansas, received an ovation for a performance at the Metropolitan Opera in New York.

Newport suffered a $1 million fire, with twenty residential blocks burning. Two fires at Conway burned 7,500 bales of cotton.

John E. Martineau defeated Tom J. Terral in the race for governor.

Citizens of Almyra donated 160 acres for use as a rice branch experiment station for the University of Arkansas.

A Thanksgiving Day tornado killed fifteen persons in Heber Springs and property destruction was reported from a wide area.

1927

Nearly one hundred persons in Arkansas lost their lives in floods in different sections of the state as heavy rainfall caused streams and rivers to leave their banks. Part of the Baring Cross Bridge was carried away by flood waters. Herbert Hoover visited here in connection with relief work for flood sufferers.

Charles A. Lindbergh visited the state and was viewed by thousands.

E. L. McHaney was appointed to the Supreme Court after Justice Hart had been made chief justice to succeed A. E. McCulloch.

Little Rock High School, at Fourteenth and Park Streets, was completed and was termed "the most beautiful high school building in America." Its cost was $1.5 million. Before the new building was finished, students completed their high school education in a building now occupied by East Side Junior High School at Fourteenth and Scott Streets.

1928

Senator Joe T. Robinson was named as the Democratic nominee for vice president, appearing on the ticket with Al Smith, presidential nominee.

El Dorado completed a new city hall and municipal building.

The Arkansas State Chamber of Commerce was organized, with Harvey C. Couch elected chairman.

Governor Parnell called a special session of the legislature to enact important highway legislation.

A boys' dormitory of Henderson-Brown College was destroyed by fire. The engineering machine shop at the University of Arkansas burned with the loss estimated at $150,000.

1929

Expansions were planned for the Tuberculosis Sanatorium in Booneville and for the State Hospital for Nervous Diseases. Governor Parnell appointed a construction commission to take charge of the building program.

Purchase of a block of ground adjoining Peabody School was announced by the federal government and a new post office and federal building planned.

George W. Donaghey and Mrs. Donaghey set up a trust fund for Little Rock Junior College, presenting the college with the fourteen-story Donaghey Building and the five-story Waldon Building, both at Seventh and Main Streets.

Construction of Carpenter Dam, near Hot Springs, was planned by the Arkansas Power and Light Co. as another hydroelectric project.

1930

Serious drought severely affected crops in the state, with no rainfall for more than two summer months. Little Rock temperatures soared to 107 degrees in the parched weather.

Workmen dug a meteoric stone from the ground in Paragould and sent it to the Field Museum in Chicago.

Sam J. Wilson, an Arkansas banker, was appointed liquidating agent of the American Exchange Bank in Little Rock.

A large fire destroyed part of the town of Dover in Pope County.

A storm in Phillips County killed seventeen persons and injured one hundred.

1931

With a serious economic depression settling over the state, many thousands of citizens were thrown out of work. The Red Cross reported in January that it was providing assistance to 519,516 Arkansas persons. In England, a crowd that had gathered in the streets threatened to loot stores unless food was provided.

Airmail service was inaugurated in Little Rock.

State officials reported that $80 million had been spent in Arkansas highway construction under the Martineau building program.

Mrs. Hattie W. Caraway from Jonesboro was nominated by the Democratic State Central Committee to fill the unexpired term of her late husband, Senator T. H. Caraway.

1932

J. Marion Futrell was nominated for governor in the Democratic primary, Mrs. Hattie Caraway for senator, and Lee Cazort for lieutenant governor. The race for governor opened with the following candidates campaigning: Mr. Futrell, Dwight H. Blackwood, S. Marcus Bone, Leonard D. Caudle, Dan W. Johnston, Richard M. Mann, A. B. Priddy, Howard Reed, Tom J. Terral, Charles A. Walls, W. P. Wilson, and Alley Woodrow.

Members of the Arkansas Democratic Women's Club held their first annual convention in Lafayette Hotel.

1933

Restrictions of cotton growing were announced by agricultural officials, with 97,000 cotton acreage abandonment contracts being signed by Arkansas growers. T. Roy Reid was assistant director in charge of the state Agricultural Extension Service.

Arkansas citizens went to the polls and voted to repeal the Eighteenth Amendment by a ratio of three to two.

Eight new work camps for the Civilian Conservation Corps were built in Arkansas to serve 1,400 more CCC recruits.

A tornado that struck in Izard and Randolph Counties killed five persons and injured many others.

Federal relief provided in Arkansas in 1933 amounted to $8.4 million, it was reported by W. R. Dyess, the state administrator.

1934

A midsummer drought caused the Arkansas River to read the low mark of three feet below zero.

More than ten thousand persons heard Secretary of Agriculture Henry Wallace speak at Marianna.

The legislature cleared the way to complete construction of the Benton unit of the state hospital, which had stood in an unfinished condition for several years.

Mrs. J. F. Weinmann from Little Rock was elected national president of the United States Daughters of 1812.

1935

Citizens began paying the new 2 percent retail sales tax. Validity of the legislative act setting up the tax was upheld by the Arkansas Supreme Court.

The State Utilities Commission was set up by an act of the legislature. Named to serve were P. A. Lasley, W. N. Gladson, and Joe Bond. The Commission replaced the Fact Finding Tribunal.

1936

Seventeen persons were killed in the crash of an airliner in the woods near Goodwin in St. Francis County. Among the casualties were W. R. Dyess, WPA administrator for Arkansas, and R. H. McNair Jr., director of finance and reports. Floyd Sharp succeeded Dyess as administrator.

The city of Little Rock purchased the water supply system, issuing $6,590,000 in bonds for payment.

William H. "Coin" Harvey, advocate of bimetallism, died at his home in Monte, Nebraska.

The Democratic State Committee met in Little Rock and selected delegates to the national convention. They were instructed to vote for President Franklin D. Roosevelt and Vice President John Garner.

1937

The nation joined Arkansas in mourning the death of Senator Joseph T. Robinson, who for more than a quarter of a century dominated the political picture in this state. Thousands braved a torrid July sun to pay final homage to him. A large delegation from Washington attended the funeral services in the First Methodist Church.

Death also took George W. Donaghey, who devoted his 1909–1913 tenure of office to completion of the state's $2.5 million capitol building.

Aroused by the state Democratic committee's refusal to call a primary to select a successor to Senator Robinson, hundreds of party members met in Little Rock to name Representative John E. Miller as their independent candidate. Miller won in the special election, defeating Carl E. Bailey.

Thomas C. Trimble, a Lonoke attorney, succeeded the late John E. Martineau as federal judge.

Oil and wood brought new industrial activity to south Arkansas in 1937. The Lion Oil Refining Co. opened the deep sand Shuler Field in Union County. Other oil fields also were developed. The Crossett Lumber Co. opened a new $4 million paper mill, spotlighting the value of Arkansas forest products.

Victor A. Gates, a Little Rock landowner, was murdered after he picked up a hitchhiker along one of the state's highways, and a Lonoke jury ordered the electrocution of Lester Brockelhurst, twenty-three years old, for the slaying.

1938

Arkansas cotton farmers received cotton price-adjustment

(parity) payments amounting to $11,750,000.

The first Arkansas livestock show was held in North Little Rock, marking the initial rapid expansion of the livestock industry in the state.

Arkansas officials distributed 1,789,000 schoolbooks to students in the state during the first year of the free textbook program. Cost to the state was $662,000. The average cost for books per student was $1.66.

1939

A large-scale business development program in all industries sent employment figures to a high point.

The Cotton Belt Shops in Pine Bluff carried out an $110,000 building program.

Lloyd L. Rayburn, an escaped Texas convict, was sentenced to die for the killing of Sergeant Sigur Fosse of the US Marines in a Little Rock café in an attempted holdup.

1940

Heavy activity marked the construction of Camp Robinson, and troops began arriving late that year to start the training program for draftees who were scheduled to arrive shortly.

The 153rd Infantry Regiment, an all-Arkansas unit, was mobilized in December for a year of active training.

Industrial payrolls soared high throughout the state, sparked by large-scale military preparations and a general upswing of business conditions.

Little Rock firemen set a record for minimum fire losses for the year, the property losses amounting to only $110,000 for the entire city.

Norman Baker, operator of a hospital at Eureka Springs, was tried and convicted on a mail-fraud charge.

Plans to erect a new Pulaski County hospital were being formulated. (The hospital subsequently built on W. Roosevelt Road replaced one which stood on a site now occupied by the Westinghouse Electric Co.'s big factory.)

Little Rock's bank deposits reached $55 million, an increase of $13 million over those of the preceding year.

1941

Brigadier General F. B. Mallon was named to direct the Infantry Replacement Training program at Camp Robinson. The training program was set up following the departure of the Thirty-Fifth Division that had been at the camp nearly a year.

Production of fuses, detonators, and other war machine parts at the Arkansas Ordinance Plant was about to get under way at the end of 1941. Construction-crew payrolls amounted to $300,000 weekly at year's end. The Maumelle Ordinance Plant in Marche was 40 percent complete at year's end.

A tire-rationing program was put into effect and the procedure for establishing and operating a food stamp program was being discussed by civic officials.

A war among dairymen of Pulaski County resulted in the death of Elves Smith, aged twenty-two, who was struck by a bullet while he stood on the Upper Hot Springs highway. Some of the dairymen were attempting to halt passage of milk trucks when shots were discharged.

The number of men drafted in Arkansas by September was eleven thousand.

1942

Boys of eighteen began registering late in 1942. All other ages up to forty-five were already registered in the wartime draft that was placing thousands of men in army ranks.

A serious financial plight at the Arkansas Boys Industrial School in Pine Bluff was discovered. In December only $8,611 remained of a $33,980 appropriation that was scheduled to keep the school in operation until June 1943.

Pulaski County collected a total of $2,716,000 in taxes for the year, or $303,000 more than the amount paid in 1941. Slight tax rate increases accounted for the higher sum.

About one hundred thousand customers of the Arkansas Power and Light Co. were paid a refund of $625,000 on their light bills.

All the various phases of the home-defense project were in operation, with blackouts being conducted in principal cities of the state. An army of air-raid wardens, firefighters, and other civilian volunteers on the home front was receiving training.

1943

The Sixty-Sixth Panther Division moved into Camp Robinson, and later that year the camp was made a Branch Immaterial Replacement Training Center.

The Medical Replacement Training Center moved out. President Roosevelt visited the camp and attended Easter services in one of the chapels there.

William V. Browning, a Little Rock high school student, was acquitted on a charge of first-degree murder in connection with the death of his mother, Mrs. Julia K. Browning.

An "economy bloc" held down expenditures of the state legislature. Governor Adkins made a personal appearance before the group to request particular legislation.

The Abington antiviolence law was passed, and in another measure cities were allocated portions of the sales tax revenues.

An additional fifty-six thousand acres of leased land was added to the maneuver area of Camp Robinson.

1944

Taxicab monopoly in Little Rock was broken by a Supreme Court decision which directed the city of Little Rock to allow the North Little Rock Transportation Co. to pursue its application for a permit.

Arkansas was scheduled to receive $25 million in federal money for flood control work.

Residents watched newspapers closely for announcements concerning ration tickets. Items obtainable only with tickets included automobile tires, shoes, sugar, gasoline, and foods such as meats, cheese, butter, and fats. There was a drastic shortage of cigarettes, and popular brands were gone from the counters almost completely.

At year's end, Arkansas was working toward a goal of $44 million in the Sixth War Loan Drive, with about half that quota reached in December.

In December, Governor-elect Ben Laney appointed Jack Porter from Forrest City as director of the Arkansas State Police, and W. J. Smith from Texarkana as his executive secretary.

1945

James W. Hall, convicted slayer of his nineteen-year-old wife, and who confessed to five other murders, was Arkansas's top newsmaker in 1945. The Little Rock taxi driver confessed to killing his wife and scattering the remains near a lonely road northwest of Riverside Golf Course. He was electrocuted in January 1946.

A shakeup in the University of Arkansas coaching staff resulted in the replacement of Glen Rose by John H. Barnhill, who signed a five-year contract. The Razorback team, preseason title favorites, finished last.

Arkansas bonds were restored to the New York market's "approved list" following intensive goodwill work by state officials.

Several departments were consolidated and some personnel reductions were achieved during the year under the Laney administration.

A legislative act separated primaries for federal and state offices.

Important flood control hearings were conducted, with Arkansas being considered for many postwar flood-control projects.

1946

Proposal of the city of Little Rock to purchase the gas-distribution system of the Arkansas Louisiana Gas Co. was the subject of lively debate and closed with a heavy vote in an election, with Little Rock residents rejecting the planned purchase.

Ed Dunaway, a navy veteran, defeated Sam Robinson, incumbent for the position of Pulaski County prosecuting attorney.

The closing of Camp Robinson marked an end of the camp's wartime activities.

Westinghouse announced plans to build a giant lightbulb manufacturing plant in Little Rock.

1948

The spectacular rise of Sidney S. McMath from Hot Springs prosecuting attorney to governor capped the 1948 political news. Other top political news involved President Truman's vote majority in the state, which followed the national action in giving him his first full term.

It was a year of violence: one person was killed and the entire city of Pocahontas rocked by a gas explosion which destroyed four buildings; a coal-mine blast at Greenwood killed eight miners; and five died when a bomber plane struck a mountain in Newton County, all during February. Hail caused $1 million in damage at El Dorado in March. Fires at Searcy and Yellville cost $100,000 and $75,000, respectively, in June. Another fire in September cost Paragould property owners $100,000.

A bombshell was exploded in the state court system in January when the Arkansas Supreme Court ruled in January that the second Pulaski Chancery Court, and all the divorces it had granted, were illegal. The shock was heard around the world from persons who had gotten divorces. In April the court reversed the decision, and the divorce rate picked up again.

The first Negro to be admitted to the Arkansas Medical School, a girl, entered in August.

War Memorial Stadium went into use in September. In October the annual Arkansas livestock show set a new attendance record of 150,000.

A Christmas fire caused $150,000 damage on Little Rock's main street.

1949

President Harry S. Truman visited for the Thirty-Fifth Division reunion in June. He also dedicated the new War Memorial Stadium and Fair Park as War Memorial Park.

Tornadoes were much in the news, with fifty-five killed in a Warren tornado in January, sixteen more near Scott in March, and four others at Bald Knob in December.

Sid McMath was inaugurated governor. An Arkansas man, Frank Pace Jr., was named by Truman as national budget director.

The Arkansas Girls Industrial School was the scene of broad investigation as girl inmates rioted, with some escaping, in August. The State Hospital for Nervous Diseases buildings were labeled as death traps by a Pulaski grand jury in August.

A DeValls Bluff bank was robbed in October single-handedly by James Walden, a GI home from Germany who was captured thirty minutes later in Stuttgart. In DeValls Bluff in November, seven state hospital doctors were charged in a brawl.

The state antiviolence law during strikes was upheld by the US Supreme Court in December.

Ouachita College's Old Main building burned at a loss of $300,000 in May. Floods raged over the state in February as winter weather hit its peak.

1950

Little Rock was commended for a marked improvement in sanitary conditions in a US Public Health report released in December 1918.

Major J. D. Geiger, USPHS medical officer in charge, said sanitation inspectors had found that 44 percent of the 2,471 wells in use in the city the year before had been condemned and filled in or cemented over. In 1917, the report said, twelve thousand Little Rockians or more were using well water.

The well condemnations necessitated extension of about five miles of water mains and laterals, and boosted the number of city water users from 73 percent of the city's population in July 1917 to 86 percent in November 1918. During the same time, 935 sewer connections were made, representing some 2,085 houses linked to the city sewer system.

The *Arkansas Gazette*, known as the oldest newspaper west of the Mississippi River, and located from 1908 until its October 18, 1991, closing at the now historic Gazette Building, was for many years the newspaper of record for Little Rock and the state of Arkansas. The *Arkansas Gazette* began publication at Arkansas Post, the first capital of Arkansas Territory, on November 20, 1819. When the capital was moved to Little Rock in 1821, publisher William E. Woodruff also relocated the *Arkansas Gazette*. The newspaper was the first to report Arkansas's statehood in 1836.

After enduring twelve years of a bitter and fiercely contested newspaper war, the *Arkansas Gazette* published its final edition, ending what had become a 172-year-old business. The assets of the newspaper were sold to Walter E. Hussman Jr., publisher of the competing *Arkansas Democrat*. Hussman renamed the surviving paper the *Arkansas Democrat-Gazette*.

The surviving newspaper proclaims itself a descendant of the *Arkansas Gazette*, but this viewpoint is disputed by the 726 full-time and 1,200 part-time employees of the *Arkansas Gazette* who lost their jobs with the demise of their newspaper.

Resources

A Journey through Time
Lesson Plan
Grades 3–4

Journal Entry

How can a newspaper be important to a territory or state? What could a newspaper be used for in a particular time period? (Answers may vary.)

Objectives

English/Language Arts

–Generate questions that reflect active engagement in the text

–Question the author's purpose

–Recognize *expository* text structures which are comparative

Social Studies

–Examine different types of communication between communities in Arkansas

–Explain how communities share ideas and information with one another

Activities

English/Social Studies

Students are placed with a partner. Groups are presented with an article. The pair will discuss the author's purpose for writing the article and take note on a graphic organizer (double-sided notes). The pair will list questions they have about the situation that surrounds the article. The pair will discuss and record ideas about how communities shared ideas and information with one another in early Arkansas. The pair will take the information that they have discovered and share it with another pair of students. Pairs will discuss how the information is connected.

Assessment   **Extension/Enrichment**

English/Social Studies

A graphic organizer will display the
pair's ability to analyze the given
material.

English

Allow students to explore other articles.

Social Studies

Allow students to research early Arkansas on their own.

What strategies were used to address diverse learning styles?

Instructional Strategies

- ☐ Music/Art
- ☐ Movement
- ☐ Storytelling
- ☐ Role Play
- ☐ Novelty
- ☐ Brainstorming
- x Discussion
- ☐ Technology
- ☐ Project
- ☐ Problem Based
- x Graphic Organizers
- x Writing
- x Journaling
- ☐ Metaphor
- ☐ Simile
- ☐ Connections
- x Cooperative Learning
- ☐ Reciprocal Teaching
- ☐ Metacognition Strategies
- ☐ Mnemonic Devices
- ☐ Practice
- ☐ Multicultural Inclusion

Bloom's Taxonomy[21]

Blooms Revised Taxonomy

Higher Order thinking

Create
Design, build construct, plan produce devise

Evaluate
Check, Judge, Critique, experiment hypothesis, test, detect

Analyse
Compare, organise, question, research deconstruct outline, attribute

Apply
Do, carry out, use, run, implement

Understand
Interpret, summarise, explain, rephrase classify, infer, paraphrase, compare

Remember
Recall, list, retrieve, find, name, recognise identify, locate decribe

Lower Order Thinking

Resources:

Copies of several articles

One copy of a graphic organizer for each pair

Reflections:

---

21 Lauren W. Anderson and David R. Krathwohl, eds., *A Taxonomy for Learning, Teaching, and Assessing: A Revision of Bloom's Taxonomy of Educational Objectives, Abridged Edition*, Pearson, 2001.

A Journey through Time
Lesson Plan
Grades 5–6

Journal Entry

How can you participate in government at the local or national level? Explain your reasoning.

Objectives

English/Language Arts

–Identify cause/effect and problem/solution relationships
–Compare/contrast information from multiple sources

Social Studies

–Discuss ways citizens participate in government at the state and local levels
–Analyze the importance of citizen participation in government at the state and local levels

Activities

English/Social Studies

Students should be grouped in threes. Students will identify articles that address the politics involved with statehood. Students will use the articles as a springboard to develop teams of citizens that will be responsible for informing the people of current events that are keeping Congress from making Arkansas a state.

Assessment   Extension
English/Social Studies

Students will create a flyer, advertisement for the newspaper, or write a letter to Congress that expresses the feelings of the people. Groups will present the finished products.

What strategies were used to address diverse learning styles?

Instructional Strategies

- ☐ Music/Art
- ☐ Movement
- ☐ Storytelling
- x Role Play
- ☐ Novelty
- x Brainstorming
- x Discussion
- ☐ Technology
- ☐ Project
- x Problem Based
- ☐ Graphic Organizers
- x Writing
- x Journaling
- ☐ Metaphor
- ☐ Simile
- ☐ Connections
- x Cooperative Learning
- ☐ Reciprocal Teaching
- ☐ Metacognition Strategies
- ☐ Mnemonic Devices
- ☐ Practice
- ☐ Multicultural Inclusion

Bloom's Taxonomy

Blooms Revised Taxonomy

Higher Order thinking

Create
Design, build construct, plan produce devise

Evaluate
Check, Judge, Critique, experiment hypothesis, test, detect

Analyse
Compare, organise, question, research deconstruct outline, attribute

Apply
Do, carry out, use, run, implement

Understand
Interpret, summarise, explain, rephrase classify, infer, paraphrase, compare

Remember
Recall, list, retrieve, find, name, recognise identify, locate decribe

Lower Order Thinking

Resources:
Copies of several articles
Rubric for oral presentation

Reflections:

A Journey through Time
Lesson Plan
Grades 7–8

Journal Entry

Can you imagine living in Arkansas before statehood? How would your life be different from what it is now? Be very descriptive when making your comparison.

Objectives

English

–Create a draft for expository writing

–Analyze selections through text, images, and photographs for a given purpose

–Contribute appropriately to class discussion

Social Studies

–Examine the preterritorial periods of Arkansas through images

Activities

English/Social Studies

Students will work with a partner and analyze one of the illustrations from *Epic of Arkansas.*

Using the photo-analysis worksheet, students will analyze the illustration of choice with a partner.

Students will be engaged in discussion while analyzing the image.

Assessment

Extension

English/Social Studies

Students will complete the graphic organizer to analyze the image. Discussion between the students will be observed by teacher.

Read *Epic of Arkansas* and present information found with class.

What strategies were used to address diverse learning styles?

Instructional Strategies

☐ Music/Art
☐ Movement
☐ Storytelling
☐ Role Play
☐ Novelty
☐ Brainstorming
x Discussion
☐ Technology
☐ Project
☐ Problem Based
x Graphic Organizers
x Writing
x Journaling
☐ Metaphor
☐ Simile
☐ Connections
x Cooperative Learning
☐ Reciprocal Teaching
☐ Metacognition Strategies
☐ Mnemonic Devices
☐ Practice
☐ Multicultural Inclusion

Blooms Taxonomy

Resources:

Reflection:

Articles

Name_____ Date_____Class_____

Two-Column Graphic Organizer

Topic	Notes from Discussion

History Role Play: Arkansas Should Be a State by Now!

Teacher Name: _____

Student Name: _____

CATEGORY	4	3	2	1
Historical Accuracy	All historical information appeared to be accurate and in chronological order.	Almost all historical information appeared to be accurate and in chronological order.	Most of the historical information was accurate and in chronological order.	Very little of the historical information was accurate and/or in chronological order.
Role	Point of view, arguments, and solutions proposed were consistently in character.	Point of view, arguments, and solutions proposed were often in character.	Point of view, arguments, and solutions proposed were sometimes in character.	Point of view, arguments, and solutions proposed were rarely in character.
Knowledge Gained	Can clearly explain several ways in which his character "saw" things differently than other characters and can clearly explain why.	Can clearly explain several ways in which his character "saw" things differently than other characters.	Can clearly explain one way in which his character "saw" things differently than other characters.	Cannot explain one way in which his character "saw" things differently than other characters.

Props/ Costume	Student uses several props (could include costume) that accurately fit the period, show considerable work/ creativity, and make the presentation better.	Student uses one or two props that accurately fit the period and make the presentation better.	Student uses one or two props which make the presentation better.	The student uses no props or the props chosen detract from the presentation.
Required Elements	Student included more information than was required.	Student included all information that was required.	Student included most information that was required.	Student included less information than was required.

Photo Analysis Worksheet
Step 1. Observation

A.   Study the photograph for two minutes. Form an overall impression of the photograph and then examine individual items. Next, divide the photo into quadrants and study each section to see what new details become visible.

_____

B.   Use the chart below to list people, objects, and activities in the photograph.

People	Objects	Activities

Step 2. Inference

Based on what you have observed above, list three things you might infer from this photograph.

_____
_____
_____

Step 3. Questions

A.   What questions does this photograph raise in your mind?

_____
_____

B.   Where could you find answers to them?

_____
_____

Student Evaluation Worksheet

Name_____ Date_____Class_____

K	W	L

NAME _____ CLASS _____ DATE _____

Graphic Organizer

Cause and Effect Diagram

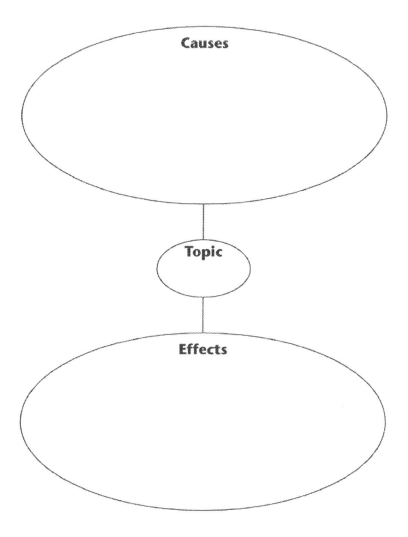

NAME _____ CLASS _____ DATE _____

Graphic Organizer
Venn Diagram

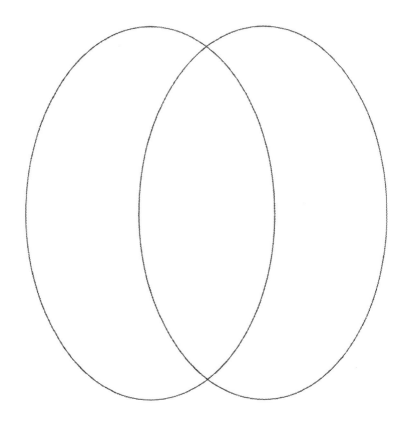

NAME _____ CLASS _____ DATE _____

Graphic Organizer

All-purpose Planner

THESIS

↓

KEY POINT ONE:	KEY POINT TWO:	KEY POINT THREE:

↓ ↓ ↓

SUPPORT	SUPPORT	SUPPORT

SUPPORT	SUPPORT	SUPPORT

Story Map

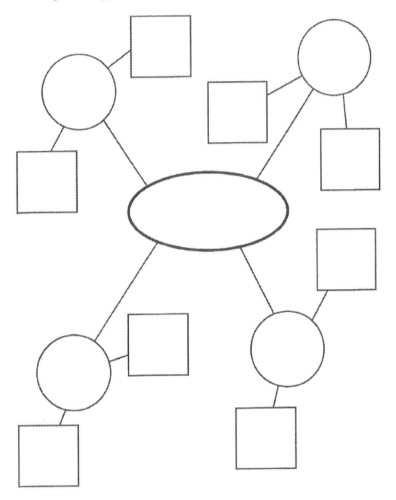

Correlation of Arkansas State Standards

Page #	Topic	Strand/ Standard	Student Learning Expectation
14	Arkansas before statehood	History	H.6.K.3 H.6.4.3 H.6.4.10
18	How Arkansas became a state	History	H.6.4.3
22	A free state or not?	History	H.6.5.21
24	The Constitutional Convention	Civics/ government	C.4.5.1
33	Work of the legislature	Civics/ government	C.4.5.5
35	The Constitutional Convention meets	Civics/ government	C.4.5.5
71	Statehood and politics	Process to achieve statehood	TP.4.AH.7-8.7

Common Core State Standards for English

Key Ideas and Details

- Cite textual evidence to support analysis of what the text says explicitly as well as inferences drawn from the text.
- Cite several pieces of textual evidence to support analysis of what the text says explicitly as well as inferences drawn from the text.
- Cite the textual evidence that most strongly supports an analysis of what the text says explicitly as well as inferences drawn from the text.
- Determine a central idea of a text and how it is conveyed through particular details; provide a summary of the text distinct from personal opinions or judgments.
- Determine two or more central ideas in a text and analyze their development over the course of the text; provide an objective summary of the text.
- Determine a central idea of a text and analyze its development over the course of the text, including its relationship to supporting ideas; provide an objective summary of the text.
- Analyze in detail how a key individual, event, or idea is introduced, illustrated, and elaborated on in a text (e.g., through examples or anecdotes).
- Analyze the interactions between individuals, events, and ideas in a text (e.g., how ideas influence individuals or events, or how individuals influence ideas or events).
- Analyze how a text makes connections among and distinctions between individuals, ideas, or events (e.g., through comparisons, analogies, or categories).
- Determine the meaning of words and phrases as they are used in a text, including figurative, connotative, and technical meanings.

- Determine the meaning of words and phrases as they are used in a text, including figurative, connotative, and technical meanings; analyze the impact of a specific word choice on meaning and tone.
- Determine the meaning of words and phrases as they are used in a text, including figurative, connotative, and technical meanings; analyze the impact of specific word choices on meaning and tone, including analogies or allusions to other texts.
- Analyze how a particular sentence, paragraph, chapter, or section fits into the overall structure of a text and contributes to the development of the ideas.
- Analyze the structure an author uses to organize a text, including how the major sections contribute to the whole and to the development of the ideas.
- Analyze in detail the structure of a specific paragraph in a text, including the role of particular sentences in developing and refining a key concept.
- Determine an author's point of view or purpose in a text and explain how it is conveyed in the text.
- Determine an author's point of view or purpose in a text and analyze how the author distinguishes his or her position from that of others.
- Determine an author's point of view or purpose in a text and analyze how the author acknowledges and responds to conflicting evidence or viewpoints.
- Integrate information presented in different media or formats (e.g., visually, quantitatively) as well as in words to develop a coherent understanding of a topic or issue.
- Compare and contrast a text to an audio, video, or multimedia version of the text, analyzing each medium's portrayal of the subject (e.g., how the delivery of a speech affects the impact of the words).

- Evaluate the advantages and disadvantages of using different mediums (e.g., print or digital text, video, multimedia) to present a particular topic or idea.
- Trace and evaluate the argument and specific claims in a text, distinguishing claims that are supported by reasons and evidence from claims that are not.
- Trace and evaluate the argument and specific claims in a text, assessing whether the reasoning is sound and the evidence is relevant and sufficient to support the claims.
- Delineate and evaluate the argument and specific claims in a text, assessing whether the reasoning is sound and the evidence is relevant and sufficient; recognize when irrelevant evidence is introduced.
- Compare and contrast one author's presentation of events with that of another (e.g., a memoir written by and a biography on the same person).
- Analyze how two or more authors writing about the same topic shape their presentations of key information by emphasizing different evidence or advancing different interpretations of facts.
- Analyze a case in which two or more texts provide conflicting information on the same topic and identify where the texts disagree on matters of factor interpretation.

Range of Reading and Level of Text Complexity

- By the end of the year, read and comprehend literary nonfiction in the grades 6–8 text complexity band proficiently, with scaffolding as needed at the high end of the range.
- By the end of the year, read and comprehend literary nonfiction at the high end of the grades 6–8 text complexity band independently and proficiently.[22]

---

[22] T. Evers, "Common Core Standards for English Language Arts," Wisconsin Department of Public Instructions, http://dpi.wi.gov/sites/default/files/imce/commoncore/pdf/ele-stds-app-a-revision.pdf.

Bibliography

Anderson, Lauren W., and David R. Krathwohl, eds. *A Taxonomy for Learning, Teaching, and Assessing: A Revision of Bloom's Taxonomy of Educational Objectives, Abridged Edition.* Pearson, 2001.

Benton, Thomas. *Thirty Years' View.* New York: D. Appleton and Co., 1883.

Center for Arkansas History and Culture. University of Arkansas at Little Rock. *Arkansas Gazette State Centennial Edition: 1836–1936.* Little Rock: Gazette Publishing, 1936.

The Encyclopedia of Arkansas History and Culture. Butler Center for Arkansas Studies at the Central Arkansas Library System. Accessed March 20, 2015. http://www.encyclopediaofarkansas.net.

Evers, T. "Common Core Standards for English Language Arts." Wisconsin Department of Public Instructions. http://dpi.wi.gov/sites/default/files/imce/commoncore/pdf/ele-stds-app-a-revision.pdf.

Novak, Fred, and John L. Novak. *The History of Arkansas.* Little Rock: Rose Publishing, 1987.

Register of Debates in Congress. Washington, DC: Gales & Seaton, 1837.

Turner, Jesse. "The Constitution of 1836." *Publications of the Arkansas Historical Association, Volume 3.*

Printed in the United States
By Bookmasters